TRUCKMAKERS™

Colin Peck

# DAF

## TRUCKS since 1949

VELOCE™

# Contents

# Foreword

## The history of the future

On April 1 1928, Hub van Doorne started a small engineering business and blacksmith workshop. Together with his brother, Wim, he laid the foundations for DAF (a PACCAR company since 1996) as a leading truck manufacturer.

Even in the early years, the activities of the Van Doorne brothers were governed by an important principle: meet the highest quality standards and the customers' needs. Many hundreds of ideas and innovations have been developed and marketed by DAF over the years. The continuously variable transmission is far and away the best-known, but whether it was the spring brake cylinder – a true DAF invention – or the turbo intercooling system first used in truck applications by DAF, all had one thing in common: they offered added value to the customer. Without exception, every innovation represented a transport solution that assisted customers in organising their transport business as efficiently and easily as possible.

This principle remains an integral part of the company's philosophy today. Low costs per kilometre, and the highest possible productivity and vehicle availability are the company's key values, in combination with best-in-class driver comfort. These have always been the driving forces behind our development activities, and in the future, too, DAF will continue to give these the highest priority.

I would like to compliment author Colin Peck for writing this book, which does full justice to DAF's rich industrial heritage. At the same time, it is a tribute to all those thousands of employees who contributed and still contribute to the success of our company with their expertise, creativity, dedication and drive for quality.

**Aad L Goudriaan**
**President DAF Trucks NV**

# Introduction

My involvement with the transport industry goes back a long way. I worked in transport management in the UK during the late 1960s and throughout the 1970s, and then as a freelance correspondent for trucking magazines in the UK, America, Australia, Canada and South Africa during the 1970s and 1980s.

Since the early 1980s I've been involved in the classic car industry, collecting and restoring old cars, running classic car clubs and writing the occasional feature about my interests. However, my profession as a public relations consultant has seen me recently return to the commercial vehicle arena and renew my involvement with DAF trucks. During my research into the marque, I discovered that there had not been any sizeable historical publication on DAF, in English, in almost 30 years, so this book goes some way to putting that right.

Obviously there are size constraints on publishing a book such as this, and the sheer volume and quality of material that my research unearthed could easily have generated a book several times the size of this one. So, editing down the material and making a final selection of images has been difficult indeed, but I hope that the content goes some way towards scratching the surface of the legacy of this outstanding truck manufacturer.

I hope you have as much fun reading this volume as I did researching and writing it.

**Colin Peck**
**Wraysbury, England**

# Acknowledgements

This book is a tribute to the many DAF employees, past and present, without whose help this book would not have been possible. I would also like to express my gratitude for the exceptional help I received from DAF marketing teams in Holland, the UK and Australia, as well as the amazing efforts of archivists Wim and Jo at the DAF museum in Eindhoven, without whose support this book would be a very thin volume indeed.

I would like to acknowledge the help of operators, dealers, journalists, drivers and enthusiasts from around the world, who contributed material, data, photos and anecdotes from their DAF experiences. It won't be possible to mention everybody who has had a part in making this book possible, but I will list as many as I can:

Harm Adams
Rob Appels (DAF NL)
John Beveridge
Big Lorry Blog (UK)
Ferry Bosman
Jerry Burley
Mike Carnevale
Max Chern

Bill Clowes
Lee Coulson
*Diesel* magazine (Aus)
Mike Glendinning
Clara Hornley (PACCAR Aus)
Hans Houtsma
Niels Jansen
Peter Jackson
Caspar Lecluse
Jo Louvenberg
Roy Mead
Richard Mohr
*NZ Trucking* magazine
Tony Pain (DAF UK)
Colin Ryan
Rod Simmonds
David Skinner
Hans Staals
Richard Stanier
Peter Symons
*Truckin Life* magazine (Aus)
Jeroen Vossen
Wim Zelders

# History of DAF – setting the wheels in motion

Hubertus Josephus van Doorne was clearly marked for 20th century greatness by being born on the very first day of the new century, January 1 1900, in America, a small village in Limburg, Holland. Despite his humble upbringing as the eldest son of the village blacksmith, he was destined to become one of the most imaginative vehicular engineers of the 20th century.

By the mid 1920s, having been turned down for employment at the Philips electrical company, Hub had worked his way up to foreman in the small engineering works of Sjef Mandigers in Eindhoven. This was where he came in contact with Mr Huenges, proprietor of the Coolen brewery and ice factory, who owned a splendid Stearns-Knight automobile with a sleeve valve engine. When the car developed an engine knock that the dealer could not cure, Hub proved to be the only person with the skills to fix it. Huenges was so impressed by Hub's technical capabilities that on 1 April 1928 he offered Hub financial support to the tune of 10,000 Dutch guilders, to help him set up in business.

Combining Hub's imaginative engineering talents with the commercial management skills of his younger sibling, Wilhelmus, the brothers opened a small engineering workshop known as Van Doorne's Machinefabriek, producing ladder frames, ladders and metal cabinets in Eindhoven, in the south of Holland.

The van Doornes' business began with four employees in a small workshop in a corner of the brewery. The business focused on welding, engineering and forging work, including repairs for the canal boats that called at Eindhoven. The combination of Hub and Wim's complementary skills saw the business flourish, and the loan from Huenges was soon paid back.

Within a year the company had grown to the point where it employed 32 people, and two years later, now managed by Wim, it began manufacturing a range of commercial vehicle trailers and semi-trailers to take advantage of the fact that Holland was fast becoming one of Europe's most prolific road transport nations.

An innovative automatic trailer coupling was patented by Hub in 1930, and a refined version was subsequently introduced in 1934. This coupling meant that the driver did not have to leave the cab to hitch up to a trailer, as vacuum and electrical lines were connected automatically, and the landing gear was raised hydraulically. In addition, the tractor unit did not need to couple in a straight line to the trailer, but could couple from any angle up to 90 degrees.

Following the success of the new trailer designs the company name was changed, in 1931, to Van Doorne's Aanhangwagenfabriek NV (which translates to Van Doorne's trailer factory). The name was too long and unwieldy for most customers, who just started referring to the company by its initials: DAF.

At the 1934 Amsterdam Show, Hub exhibited a new design of trailer that he had been perfecting the previous year. He called it the DAF featherweight trailer, and although it was no means as light as the name implied, it was estimated to be at least 40 percent lighter than other similar capacity trailers on the market. Not only did this produce useful payload and profit gains for hauliers, but it also provided cost-savings for the company, by virtue of using fewer raw materials to construct it.

DAF 5-ton trailer delivered in 1932. (Courtesy DAF Museum)

As a result, the featherweight was an instant success. Hauliers from all over northern Europe made the trip to the small factory at Eindhoven, seeking to improve the efficiency of their operations by using lightweight DAF trailers. Such was the demand for the new trailer designs that lightweight trailers of all shapes and sizes were now being built at the DAF workshop, and in a single year almost 400 large trailers were constructed. By 1935 the company was employing some 100 people, a number that would triple over the next five years.

However, despite the success of the DAF trailer business, both Hub and Wim had a secret desire to build a DAF motor vehicle – although with Europe flooded at the time by cheap mass-produced American imports, the brothers knew that competition would be fierce.

As word spread across Europe of the inventive genius

of the van Doorne concern, Captain Van der Trappen, of the Dutch army artillery, approached Hub and asked if he could come up with a cheap, simple and reliable means of making light commercial vehicles more suitable for off-road travel. The Captain reasoned that should there be an outbreak of hostilities in Europe, large numbers of lightweight vehicles with off-road capabilities might be more effective than small numbers of specialised fighting vehicles.

The concept intrigued the van Doornes, and Hub set about designing a solution, which he called the 'Trado drive' (named as an amalgamation of Trappen and Doorne). This was a bogie arrangement, fitted in place of the axle hubs and brakes to create a double-drive unit. This enabled a 4x2 vehicle to be easily converted into a 6x4, and seemed to be an effective way of producing off-road vehicles during a period when there was insufficient funding from the Dutch armed forces to purchase the necessary all-wheel drive vehicles. As a result many army vehicles were retrofitted with the DAF Trado drive system.

Unfortunately, when hostilities did eventually break out, the sheer power and might of the aggressor proved that Van der Trappen had been right all along, but the authorities had waited too long to come to a decision to buy in large quantities. However, that's another story ...

With the clouds of war forming over Europe in the late 1930s, the Dutch government negotiated the manufacture, under licence, of Humber armoured cars. DAF was asked to undertake the work, but Hub reckoned that he could come up with a more effective design.

The resulting DAF design, known as the M-39 armoured car, proved to be the most advanced of its kind in the world, and many of its principles were to be adopted years later in Soviet tanks. Inwardly, though, Hub was saddened that the first complete vehicle that DAF built should be used for war.

Trials of the M-39 proved so successful that Britain sought to build it under licence. However, the outbreak of war swiftly curtailed those plans, and in the end only some 20 were built in Holland before the country was overrun by invading German forces. Some M-39s were used to defend against the Germans, but the remaining vehicles were taken over and used initially for policing duties. Eventually they were sent into battle on the eastern front, and were subsequently destroyed by Russian forces.

The invasion of Holland effectively brought about the cessation of engineering work at the Eindhoven factory. Although the German aviation ministry in Berlin took control of the plant and drafted in pilot-engineer H Bröcker to run things, the DAF workforce adopted a policy of non-cooperation.

The company did build some steel hardware for tank defences, and the occasional trailer or portable building, as well as carrying out repairs on trucks and trailers under German supervision. But ultimately the Eindhoven workforce proved so unproductive that, thankfully, the allies never thought the factory important enough to warrant an air raid. However, DAF also cleverly used this time to develop two prototype trucks: the DT5, a five-ton chassis; and the DT10, a ten-ton chassis. Needless to say, this was a project that Bröcker took much interest in.

The DT5 was powered by a Burmeister & Wain diesel engine, while the DT10 acquired a Deutz unit. Parts for both were very hard to come by, and had to be sanctioned directly by Berlin. In fact, such were the shortages of components that the unit in the DT5 was one of a consignment that was meant to power generator sets destined for the German army.

Meanwhile, the van Doorne brothers refused to allow their talents to be used by the invading forces. They cleverly got a local physician to prescribe them both a long period of rest. And rest they did ... but they were certainly far from idle. Hub rigged his home with an elaborate system to warn of approaching intruders, and behind its closed doors the brothers worked on plans to contribute to Holland's recovery once the war was over.

It seemingly never occurred to the van Doornes that the allies might not win the war, and the plans conceived in those dark days of the early 1940s included the creation of a Dutch motor industry, the likes of which the nation had never before seen.

Some of DAF's first vehicles were a batch of trolleybuses delivered to Groningen in 1947.
(Courtesy DAF Museum)

In the immediate postwar years, as workers trickled back to the factory from various locations, including prison camps and front-line battalions alongside allied troops, they found few raw materials to work with. Even basic building materials were scarce. The Dutch government, newly returned from its self-imposed exile in Britain, was keen for the van Doornes to push ahead with their plans to create a Dutch automotive industry, but the brothers argued that the time wasn't yet right. They reasoned that it was better for DAF to concentrate on its traditional products and build the company back up to a sound economic position, before taking the major step toward vehicle production. Europe was also flooded with large numbers of army surplus vehicles, so there was little immediate need for extra ones.

There was, however, a huge demand for transport equipment to help with the reconstruction of the Netherlands. The series production of trailers and semi-trailers became the first priority for DAF, while the engineering department started work on its first bus designs, and, in response to questions first raised behind closed doors in 1943, the company drew up plans for a trolleybus chassis.

The first batch of trolleybuses was produced in 1947 for the city of Groningen. They were bodied by Verheul, a Dutch coachbuilder that became a subsidiary of British Leyland in the 1960s, before the factory burnt down in 1970.

DAF was also involved in the construction of a large number of passenger-carrying trailers, mainly for Dutch State Railways and its associate companies. Although these trailers were later banned under Dutch traffic laws, they did carry millions of people to work each day, and they played a major role in helping the country's trade and industry start moving again.

The van Doornes worked on numerous new projects in the immediate postwar period, including building several types of jet aircraft fast-refuelling trailers, some of which were ordered by the United States airforce stationed in Holland. They also engineered a novel concept of mounting bus engines on sliding rails so that they could be easily accessed for maintenance.

11

DAF was also involved in the construction of large numbers of passenger-carrying trailers, mainly for Dutch State Railways and its associate companies. (Courtesy Niels Jansen collection)

However, the brothers were much busier behind the scenes, negotiating with the Dutch ministry of trade to decide how much government finance could be added to DAF's own resources in order to build and equip a new plant dedicated to vehicle production. While negotiations were taking place, Hub was busy finalising the designs of the very

first DAF trucks, which were launched in September 1949. Needless to say, these first DAF production trucks were loosely based on the DT5 prototype, built during the war years, which had travelled more than 100,000km without any major problems.

The 3.5-ton capacity A-30 and the 5-ton A-50 were the

Early DAF with coachbuilt cab. (Courtesy DAF Museum)

first trucks off the line, quickly followed by the 6-ton A-60 and the K-40 tractor unit, the latter of which had a gross train weight of up to 13 tons, depending on the engine fitted.

These first trucks were assembled in small numbers using components brought in from other manufacturers. Imported Hercules 4014cc JXE3 six-cylinder petrol engines, producing 91bhp, were chosen for the lighter trucks, whilst the more powerful 4620cc, 102bhp JXC unit was used in the heavier chassis, which proved an ideal choice, as there were hoards of spare parts available from ex-military sales. The British-built 83bhp Perkins P6 was the diesel option. Axles were sourced from Timken, and cabs were initially constructed by local coachbuilders.

1949 DAF T-50 with coachbuilt cab. (Courtesy DAF Museum)

# The 1950s – new factories, new trucks and buses

Most of the first DAF trucks, introduced at the end of 1949, were produced at the old trailer works and supplied to the Dutch army. Initially, DAF only provided a powered chassis, with an all-steel cab available as a 1400 Dutch guilder option. This allowed buyers to get local coachbuilders to build truck cabs, as well as bodies, for an all-inclusive price. The all-steel cab was to become a standard fitment in 1951.

With the formation of NATO, and its coordinated defence plans for the region, the Dutch government asked DAF to start production of a new all-wheel-drive military vehicle. Whilst DAF would normally have welcomed such an order with open arms, the problem was that both existing DAF factories were running at full capacity. So where could these military trucks be built?

1950 T-60. (Courtesy DAF Museum)

By 1951, DAF was producing more than 1000 trucks a year at Eindhoven. (Courtesy DAF Museum)

1952 T-60. (Courtesy DAF Museum)

The answer was to build a vast new factory, comprising 60,000 square metres of floor space, with much of the funding coming from the USA. The damage done to property and infrastructure during WWII was immense, and so the United States developed a plan for rebuilding and creating a stronger foundation for the countries of Western Europe, whilst at the same time helping to repel communism. This was named the Marshall Aid Plan, after the US Secretary of State, George Marshall.

During the period the plan was active, some $13 billion in economic aid and technical assistance was given to help the recovery of Western European countries. The Dutch government was quick to seize on the opportunity by acquiring sufficient funding for a large order of military 4x4 and 6x4 trucks from DAF in 1952. This was a significant turning point for the development of DAF as a major motor vehicle manufacturer, and laid firm foundations for its continued success.

By this time the Eindhoven plant was turning out more than 1000 trucks a year. However, a new dilemma loomed on the horizon. By the mid 1950s every DAF truck and bus chassis that could be made was being eagerly snapped up by customers across Holland, and also in a growing number of export markets, including South America.

The Marshall Plan enabled the Dutch government to fund a large order in 1952 for 4x4 and 6x6 army trucks from DAF. (Courtesy DAF Museum)

The days of the antiquated Hercules petrol engine and the small Perkins diesel were fast coming to an end, and the van Doornes were busy exploring new sources of engines better suited to the increasing demands of their customers.

Leyland, in the UK, was producing more diesel engines than it could build chassis to install them in, so it was looking to sell these surplus engines to other truck and bus manufacturers. In Britain, manufacturers such as Bedford and Seddon were already using Leyland engines, and these had been joined in Europe by the likes of Pegaso, Scania and Sisu. So, in 1955 DAF struck a deal with Leyland, whereby

DAF would buy Leyland engines and ultimately build them under licence.

This enabled DAF to begin phasing out the Hercules petrol engines and standardise on diesel powerplants, such as the 105bhp SAE Leyland 0.350 and the 108bhp SAE Perkins R6 diesels. However, although the Perkins P6 engine established a good reputation, its successor, the R6, proved problematic, and its installation was quickly dropped – thus DAF continued using the 83bhp P6 in limited numbers until 1962.

A number of major milestones were achieved during

1956 V1500 4x4. (Courtesy DAF Museum)

1955, including the completion of the 10,000th civilian truck chassis in May, whilst October saw the delivery of the 5000th military vehicle to the Dutch army. At the same time, the company also introduced the C-cabbed 1100, 1300 and 1500 series, which now featured a revised chrome grille with the number of horizontal slats reduced from seven to six.

The introduction of the imported 5760cc, Leyland 0.350 105bhp six-cylinder diesel had proven an outstanding success for DAF. However, as both Leyland and DAF increased production of trucks, there was a question over whether available supplies of UK-built engines could meet this new demand.

Therefore, in 1956, DAF began work on the construction of its own engine production plant, and by the summer of the following year batches of its first engine, the DD575 (5.75 litres) – based on the Leyland 0.350 – were being built to supplement the supply of engines imported from the UK. The DAF-built engines produced 120bhp SAE, and this overcame engine supply problems and allowed DAF

In 1957 DAF introduced its first bonneted trucks, generically known as the 'Torpedo' series. They were initially supplied in chassis and bonnet form to allow coachbuilders to build their own cabs.
(Courtesy DAF Museum)

Torpedo 6x4 dump truck, complete with DAF's in-house cab introduced in 1958. This particular example started out as a 4x2 truck, but the owner had an REO tandem rear axle setup added to increase payload capacity. (Courtesy Niels Jansen collection)

to ramp up production of truck and bus chassis even further.

To meet the more conservative demands of specific sectors of the market, DAF introduced its first bonneted truck in 1957, with mechanical specifications similar to the cab-over-engine models. Generically known as the 'Torpedo' series, the new trucks were initially supplied as a chassis and bonnet, allowing coachbuilders to construct the cabs. However, DAF introduced versions with its own in-house cab in 1958.

The 13 and 16 series were available in various rigid 4x2 chassis configurations suitable for a variety of platform and tipper bodies. A 155bhp Hercules petrol engine was still listed as an option, as was the Perkins P6. However, the licence-built 105bhp Leyland 0.350 and DAF's own DD575 were the most popular fitments.

A 24-ton GVW 4x2 tractor unit, known as the T18 series, was also added to the range in 1959, and this featured a turbocharged 5.75-litre diesel producing 165bhp, which DAF numbered the DS575. The development of this engine

was a major milestone for DAF as it became one of the very first manufacturers to offer turbocharging as a standard fitment. Large numbers of these trucks were exported to Iran and featured Trilex wheels.

The success of the licence-built 5.75-litre engine led to strengthening markets, both at home and overseas, and DAF's engineers looked at ways of enhancing the output of the engine. Not content with just engineering a bigger capacity version (the DF615, which produced 138bhp in naturally aspirated 6.15-litre form), it was further developed for turbocharging. The result was the 168bhp SAE DT615 turbo diesel.

Whilst the family of engines developed from the licence-built 0.350 helped DAF expand its truck and bus range by leaps and bounds, the van Doornes were under no illusion that this small diesel would fulfil their vision of the future. So, a further deal was signed with Leyland, this

In 1957 DAF launched the 2000 DO series designed for cross-border trucking. It was DAF's first heavyweight truck, and was initially powered by 165bhp Leyland 0.680 engines. (Courtesy DAF Museum)

time for the larger 11.1-litre 0.680 and the Powerplus P680 engines, which in normal Leyland specifications produced between 165 and 220bhp.

Before long these 'big' Leyland diesels were rebuilt at Eindhoven, and they enabled DAF to introduce its first heavyweight truck and tractor series in 1957, known as the 2000 DO. This was designed to meet the growing requirement in international cross-border trucking, and was initially powered by 11.1-litre, 165bhp Leyland-built 0.680 engines, but subsequently by the DP 680 220bhp engine.

The 2000 DO had a 10-ton rear axle designed for operation at a gross vehicle weight of 35 tons, which was allowed in Germany and many other European countries. However, until vehicle weight regulations in Holland were brought in line with these countries, Dutch operators could not make full use of these heavyweight rear axles, and could only operate the trucks at 32 tons GVW in Holland.

Its cab was essentially a modified version of that introduced on the 1300, 1600, T1800 and 1900 series, with a large grille on the front to aid engine cooling. However, due

to a number of changes in European trucking legislation, the 2000 DO was not the great success it should have been.

Whilst DAF had originally used Timken axles and Fuller gearboxes, the company was always looking at ways to improve components, which ultimately led to their in-house manufacture. So it was no surprise that in 1958, DAF began the production of its own design of rear axles, whilst at the same time switching from Fuller to ZF gearboxes. In less than ten years the company had gone from manufacturing chassis and buying in most of the major components from third parties, to producing complete vehicles.

Having spent the latter part of the decade introducing new models and new engines to the product range, DAF rounded out the 1950s with upgrades to the 1100, 1300 and 1500 forward control models. The C-cab was given a face-lift with new grille treatment, and the range received new variants of the 575 series engine, including the turbocharged DS575, which developed 165bhp. A range-topping 1900 series was also added at the same time.

# The 1960s
# – refining the product

If the 1950s had been the founding decade for DAF trucks, then the Swinging Sixties was the period when the van Doornes further developed and refined their products and established the DAF brand as a major force on the European automotive market.

The small Leyland 0.350 and the bigger 0.680 diesels had been a great success for DAF, and not only had the company built them in Eindhoven, but from 1957 it had developed its own refined engines.

The 1960s was also the decade that witnessed exponential growth in international transport by road, as industrialists across Europe found that it was increasingly quicker and reliable to ship their products by truck, rather than by rail and ship as they had in the past. The new TIR international road haulage system created a demand for big, powerful trucks that could carry a payload of 20-25 tons in a reliable and efficient manner. Such long-haul trucks also created an increasing demand for sleeper cabs and driver comfort levels

In August 1965 a convoy of 15 trucks, including 12 DAFs (six 2000 DOs and six 2600s), plus a Daffodil car, set out on a 6000km round trip from Amsterdam to Moscow. They carried exhibition material for Dutch technical and chemical firms exhibiting at an industrial fair in the Sokolniky Park in Moscow.
(Courtesy Richard Stanier collection)

that went beyond the basic creature comforts found in most trucks of the era.

So, whilst a sleeper cab version of the 2000 DO was introduced in 1961, alongside a 6x2 AS model for heavy

haulage, the model range was expanded in 1963 with the introduction of the 2300 DO series. Both ranges shared the same cab style and Leyland 0.680 engines, but they had different axles, giving different weight categories, with the

2300 rated at up to 35 tons GVW. However, with increasing demand for innovative purpose-built models for TIR work, the 2000 and 2300 DO series were already earmarked for replacement by a new DAF truck that would set a new bench mark in trans-European haulage.

The DAF 2600 series, introduced as "The mother of international road transport," astounded the European trucking fraternity with its compact design for maximum load length and its modern cab design. Cab designer W van den Brink had managed to create a standard sleeper cab within an overall length of 1.8 metres, and it set a new standard in driver comfort.

At a stroke, the spectacular 2600 alleviated all the shortcomings of the 2000 DO, and the new truck ensured DAF's position as the market leader in driver comfort for many years to come. The trucking industry had never before seen such a well-appointed – if not luxuriously trimmed – cab, which gave a crew of two ample space and amenities for a comfortable overnight stop.

The 2600's cab was such a radical departure from the norm that it became the bench mark other manufacturers set out to emulate. Initially launched with Leyland DP680 diesels rated at 220bhp, the 2600 was to enjoy a production run of 11 years, during which time substantially more powerful engine options would become available.

The 2600 was destined to become a volume seller for DAF, and it helped the company achieve a major milestone in 1964, with the delivery of DAF's 50,000th truck chassis.

In fact, the success of the 2600 now saw DAF being viewed as comparable, in terms of quality, to established European truckmakers such as Magirus-Deutz, Mercedes-Benz, MAN, Saviem and Scania. In addition, the high standards of cab comfort that the new 2600 had set were not seen as only for long-haul drivers; they were also demanded by drivers of more humble daily delivery trucks.

So, throughout the 1960s DAF was constantly revising and upgrading its range of daily delivery and construction trucks, which would ultimately lead to the introduction of a brand new range of modular cab designs. The cab of the flagship 2600 was given a face-lift in 1965, gaining a new interior for increased comfort, plus a new driveline for increased performance.

The availability of a 13-ton rear axle generated models suitable for operation at 36-40 tons GVW, and the newly improved 2000, 2300 and 2600 series were then used to spearhead a sales drive into neighbouring France and Belgium. This expansion programme was further

Introduced in 1964, the 2600 set a new bench mark in long-haul trucking.
(Courtesy Roy Mead)

1600 series 4x2 and drawbar trailer. (Courtesy Niels Jansen)

facilitated by the opening of a 53,000 square metre cab and axle assembly plant in the Belgian town of Westerlo.

Whilst new models, markets and plants made the news, another major event occurred in 1965 that was to have a profound effect on the company's future. It was the year that Hub van Doorne – founder and engineering genius behind the DAF product – reached pensionable age and retired from the company, his place at the helm being taken by Wim.

The following year, DAF decided to begin exporting trucks to the UK, and two distributors were appointed: the Chipping Sodbury Motor Company Ltd to cover the south of the country, and the Ackworth Engineering Co Ltd, based near Pontefract, to cover the north. Despite a shortage of new trucks on the British market at that time, DAF sales were initially restricted because of the lack of a comprehensive nationwide dealer support network, but this was to change within a few years.

The mid-1960s was also a period when DAF placed much emphasis on the development of models specifically designed for the construction industry. In 1965 DAF introduced its first 6x6 tipper chassis, the AZ 1900DS,

1900AS 6x2. (Courtesy Niels Jansen)

followed a year later by the extra-heavy duty ATE 2400 6x4 chassis, built especially for export to European countries and beyond.

However, DAF never lost its core focus on its delivery and long-haul trucks, and to support its increasing sales into the international haulage sector further variations on the flagship 2600 theme were introduced in 1967, with trailing axle (AS) 6x2 and double-drive (AT) 6x4 configurations being launched. In addition, the heavy end of the DAF product range was further enhanced, in 1968, with the introduction of a new series of DAF-developed 11.6-litre naturally aspirated engines, known as the K-series. The DK 1160 produced 230bhp SAE, whilst the DKA 1160 made ingenious use of tuned-length induction ram-pipes to boost the peak output to 250bhp. Both were naturally aspirated units.

The introduction of these new high-capacity engines at the 1968 Amsterdam RAI exhibition tended to overshadow the unveiling of the prototype of the brand new, mid range, 8.25-litre DH825 cross-flow engine that DAF's engineers were developing, and which would finally become available two years later.

# The 1970s – new cabs, new engines, and new partners

The 1970s heralded in a whole new era for DAF as the winds of change began to blow through the company. New trucks, new engines, new markets, new partners, and, perhaps most importantly, new management – a combination that was to have a long-lasting effect on the Eindhoven firm. Whilst the company had made a foray into the UK during the 1960s, the new decade kicked off with a serious effort to break into the UK truck market via a new division of DAF's UK car importers, DAF Motors of Feltham.

Whilst the old-style, normal-control bonneted trucks had been phased out, their demise was followed by the introduction of a brand new generation of trucks. DAF had been working throughout the late 1960s on the design of an innovative and modular tilt cab, which not only allowed greater access for servicing major mechanical components, but used standard pressings that could ultimately be adapted for the widest range of applications. The first incarnation of the new tilt cab was the F218 (2.18 metre wide version), which was launched at the beginning of 1970 on the brand new 1600 and 2000 series of medium weight rigid trucks and tractor units.

Not content with setting a new bench mark in cab

The first incarnation of DAF's new tilt cab appeared on the F2000 drawbar outfit. (Courtesy Peter Symons)

construction, DAF also used the models to launch a brand new 8.25-litre series engine. In the early 1960s it had become evident to DAF engineers that a new 'mid-size' engine was needed as part of the future truck programme. They had successfully managed to extract 168bhp from the turbocharged DT615 engine, whose roots went back to

25

the DD575, but they needed an engine to bridge the gap between this and the much more powerful 1160 series.

So, the engineers at Eindhoven chose a size almost exactly halfway between the two existing engines: 8.25 litres. The new engine was designed from the outset for the loadings and cooling requirements of high pressure turbocharging, and the first incarnations appeared as the 163bhp, naturally aspirated DH825, and the turbocharged DHB, producing 218bhp SAE.

Running in tandem with the boom in international truck transportation was the desire for increased gross vehicle weights, with some countries being more liberal than others in their interpretation. Harmonisation of engine power measurement scales was also wanted, alongside the introduction of minimum engine bhp per ton legislation.

Therefore, in 1971 Britain introduced regulation BSAa 141, which set the legal minimum at 6bhp per ton. This equated to a minimum of 192bhp for the then maximum allowed GVW of 32 tons, effectively creating a two-tier market whereby lightweight tractors, with barely more than the minimum required power, were the mainstay of local and day trunking operations, whilst higher-specification heavyweight tractors, usually with more than 250bhp, were the vehicles of choice for long-haul and international trucking operators. 1971 was also the year that Wim van Doorne, the business brains behind the company, followed his brother Hub into retirement.

In 1972 DAF introduced its second range of trucks with the F218 cab, designated the 2200 series. Designed to operate at up to 32 tons GVW, they were available with 180, 201 and 230bhp versions of the new 8.25-litre engine, although the higher output version proved to be the volume seller.

By 1972 the flagship 2600 was ten years old and almost on the point of being phased out, but with the introduction of 8bhp per ton legislation for operation at the 38 tons GVW allowed in Germany, DAF introduced the DKB 1160, 304bhp version of its 11.6-litre turbo diesel. The same year witnessed the setting up of DAF Trucks GB Ltd by ex-Cummins man David Mansell. This led to a significant impact on sales for the company, which at one time accounted for almost 25 per cent of truck production from Eindhoven.

The same year also saw the introduction of a new generation of lightweight 4x2 trucks with tilt cabs – the 1200DA/DD/BA and the 1400 DD/DF/BB models (cab type F198 – narrowest of the new modular cab range). They were available as a 9.5-ton GVW truck or tractor, and were powered by 5.75-litre and 6.17-litre DAF diesel options,

By 1972 the flagship 2600 was ten years old and almost on the point of being phased out. (Courtesy Roy Mead)

1972 saw the introduction of the narrowest of the new modular cabs, the F198, on the new lightweight F1200 and F1400 series. The new truck is seen here being delivered on a much modified DAF 2600 series transporter operated by de Rooy trucking, whose owner, Jan de Rooy, would later become famous for his exploits in the Paris-Dakar challenge. (Courtesy Niels Jansen)

In the 1970s, DAF provided several bus chassis for conversion to furniture trucks. This smart TB-163-based truck and trailer combination was manufactured by Carrosserie Jos Visser in The Netherlands.
(Courtesy Niels Jansen)

marriages of components, such as DAF DKA 1160-powered IH Paystar 6x4 trucks being sold in Europe, whilst Cummins E290-powered versions of DAF's soon-to-be-launched flagship 2800 series tractor were sold under the International brand in South Africa.

However, a combination of teething troubles with the 320bhp SAE DKS engine being developed for the new 2800, and the considerable investment needed for the ETD project, meant that much of the planned cash injection from IH was quickly used up, and profits dwindled. With stocks of unsold trucks piling up at Eindhoven and at dealers across Europe, profits were disappearing fast. Under the direction of one of IH's toughest marketing men, DAF recruited new marketing teams that were challenged to go out and sell trucks!

The state-owned Dutch Mining Group (DSM) already had an interest in the DAF holding company, and so took a 25 per cent holding in DAF Trucks BV. The capital injection this provided helped DAF to stage a recovery. The situation had been made worse by the car division making severe losses, although this situation eased considerably when DAF sold its car firm to Volvo in 1976, thus bringing to an end its foray into car manufacturing.

As international road transport grew, there was an increasing need for service outside of a country's borders. So, at the beginning of the '70s, DAF set up International Truck Service, or ITS, which stranded drivers could call upon for fast roadside assistance.

Despite truck sales barely reaching 12,000 units during 1973 as a result of the slump in truck sales across Europe, DAF pressed ahead with the manufacture of a truck range that was to prove beyond doubt that DAF was one of the most technically-advanced truckmakers in Europe. It was also the truck that firmly positioned DAF as a major player in the prestigious heavyweight truck category.

although 135bhp and 155bhp SAE petrol engines were also an option. However, DAF marketeers were keen to add an even smaller truck to the product range, and decided to share development costs by joining what was to become known as the 'Club of Four' agreement, with major European truck manufacturers Volvo from Sweden, Saviem from France, and Magirus from Germany, for the joint development of a new series of lightweight trucks. The project was officially known as European Truck Design (ETD) and would become fruitful within a couple of years with the launch of the F500, F700 and F900 series.

Following on from the signing of the ETD deal, DAF Trucks also signed an agreement with US truck and tractor giant International Harvester (IH) in 1973. Following IH's near-disastrous attempts to break into the European truck market under its own brand in the 1950s and 1960s, IH decided that a partnership deal offered a better chance of success, and so acquired a 33 per cent stake in DAF in return for investment capital.

The crux of the deal was intended to help DAF strengthen its financial position, whilst enabling both manufacturers to jointly develop new complementary products to sell in each other's markets. The deal did result in some unusual

The acquisition by International Harvester of a 33 per cent stake in DAF resulted in some unusual marriages of components, such as this DAF DKA 1160-powered IH Paystar 6x4. (Courtesy Niels Jansen)

Launched as a 1974 model, the F2800 became the new flagship of the range. (Courtesy Peter Symons)

Launched as a 1974 model, the F2800 was offered with a fully equipped two-bunk sleeper cab designated the F241. At 2.41 metres in width, it was the largest so far produced from the modular cab range, and whilst it was a visually impressive cab it was somewhat overshadowed by the 2800's new high-performance 1160 series diesels.

The standard tractor, designed for basic trunking work, was powered by the 260bhp turbocharged unit, whereas the top-of-the-range long-haul tractor got the 320bhp SAE DKS 1160 turbocharged and intercooled diesel – a system not used by other truck manufacturers until almost a decade later.

The new F2800 could be specified with either a 260bhp turbo diesel or a 320bhp turbocharged and intercooled 11.6-litre unit. (Courtesy Peter Symons)

The top of the range 2800 easily met requirements for German 8bhp per ton legislation, and allowed DAF to more than adequately take on competition from the likes of the 260bhp Scania 110 and the 290bhp Volvo F88. Whilst the F2800 was initially designed as a long-haul tractor unit, heavyweight rigid models such as the 8x4 FAD versions were soon added to the range. In addition to the new F241 cab being used on the F2800, DAF also supplied a number of the cabs to Hungarian truck manufacturer RABA, which used them on both rigid and tractor models.

Over in Britain it was decided to split the car (prior to its sell off) and truck sales operations into separate businesses. As a result, DAF Trucks (GB) Ltd was formed and set up in new premises in Marlow. This dynamic new venture had no history of UK sales, and therefore no baggage to carry. It was staffed by young, go-getting people with an average age of just 34, who were encouraged by senior management to 'go and do it' when it came to a deal with a customer.

## DAF model coding

| Chassis layout | Vehicle class | Drive-line |
|---|---|---|
| F: Forward control | T: Tractor Unit | T: Tandem 6x4 |
| N: Normal control | A: Long wheelbase truck | |
| | | D: Tandem 8x4 |
| | M: Mixer chassis | S: Single 6x2 |
| | | .: Single 4x2* |
| | | V: 4x4 |
| | | Z: 6x6 |
| 00: Standard chassis | 05: Heavy duty chassis | |

\* The 4x2 configuration did not have an alphanumeric code.

For example FTT 2805: forward control tractor, tandem drive 6x4, heavy duty chassis

Despite being one of the last major European truck manufacturers to enter the UK market, the company's first priority was to develop a dealer network that was the envy of most of its competitors, and this was achieved long before trucks began arriving in numbers. Being a new business in the UK, DAF was keen to dispense with the traditional view that dealers were just a means to sell trucks, and instead focussed on establishing a dealer network where they were viewed as partners.

In fact, as the manufacturer-dealer partnership matured, DAF even went so far as to ask dealer personnel to staff its stands at major motor shows from the late 1970s onwards, thus laying the foundations for excellent team building – a policy that was unheard of amongst its rivals, some of whom actively banned dealer staff from their stands unless accompanied by a customer.

As a relatively new entrant to the British truck market, DAF worked hard at building a solid reputation, and its dealers were encouraged to solve problems rather than argue with operators over who was to blame for a particular vehicle problem. Former technical engineering manager John Beveridge recalls that a problem with a DAF commercial vehicle was often turned into a positive advantage for the company.

"Our parts availability was second to none, and for the most part was to a standard almost unheard of in the British trucking industry. Our aim was to always have parts on the shelf to enable us to fix a problem and return the vehicle to service the very next day and, if need be, I could halt the production line in Eindhoven in order to obtain a part that was not available anywhere else.

"Our dedication to customer care enabled us to sell DAF vehicles with the utmost confidence that should a problem arise, we would have the parts to fix it. A perfect example of how going the extra mile on customer service reaped dividends for brand loyalty was when a relatively new coach engine suffered a major failure. On having the vehicle towed to the local DAF dealer in the UK, the operator expected the usual lengthy arguments and negotiations over blame and cost, as was the industry norm.

"However, the operator was absolutely dumbfounded when we delivered the coach back to him within 24 hours complete with a new engine. He said that no other manufacturer would have done that, and so quickly too. In fact, he was so impressed that he gratuitously told everybody in the industry that DAF had given the best service he'd ever received. Instead of arguing about it, we'd turned a negative into a positive, and this did absolute wonders for our reputation and the DAF brand."

By 1975 DAF annual truck production had reached 14,000 units. Commenting in the first ever issue of the *DAF Trucks Magazine*, I van der Putt, marketing and sales director, stated: "DAF has a secure position in the European commercial vehicle industry as a high-grade dynamic organisation with fertile ideas. It has never been possible to maintain a specifically Dutch range. The home market was just too small for that, so we had to work across the frontiers right from the start. You could say that Europe has always been our home market."

In 1975, the ETD 'Club of Four' project finally delivered a totally new range of light trucks, which although popular in mainland Europe were never sold in the UK. As a result, the small F1200 and F1400 models – introduced just three years earlier – were replaced by the ETD F700 and F900 derivatives, which would eventually cover the complete 9 to 16-ton GVW range. The cabs for the new trucks were assembled from pressings originating from the Magirus

factory in Ulm, Germany, with power coming from the DD575 120bhp engine.

The same year saw the introduction of the Supercontinental version of the F2800 series, which was basically an 'up-specced' cab package developed by DAF in the UK, specifically for operators undertaking the long-haul to the Middle East. The cab conversions were carried out by a West Country-based caravan maker. This was followed a year later by the introduction of the F2300 DHU, powered by an intercooled 8.25-litre engine developing 230bhp at 2400rpm. Some models of the F2200 were replaced by the F2300 at this time. The model, designed to slot in between the 2200 and 2800 series, was shown to the general public for the first time at the Commercial Motor Show at Earls Court, London.

The 'Club of Four' project finally matured in 1975 with the launch of the ultra-lightweight F700 and F900 trucks, featuring cabs assembled from pressings originating from Magirus.

Former fleet sales manager Peter Jackson had this to say: "In my opinion it was the F2300 that really put DAF on the map in the UK. Previous lightweight tractor units had not been volume sellers, but the F2300 was the perfect combination of lightweight tractor unit with more than adequate power and so it sold very well, even outselling the flagship F2800 series."

The company celebrated its 50th anniversary in 1978, but sadly, just one month after the celebration, Wim van Doorne passed away on 3rd May. His brother, and founder of DAF, Hub van Doorne, passed away a year later on 23rd May 1979.

The small 'Club of Four' range of lightweight trucks had been continually expanded since its introduction in 1975, and by 1978 the heaviest models in the range – the F1300 and F1500 series – had been added to the line-up. In June that year DAF also delivered the first new generation of military vehicles,

33

Launched at the Earls Court Commercial Motor Show in 1976, the 230bhp F2300 series was destined to become a volume seller for DAF. (Courtesy Peter Symons)

The F2300 FAD 8x4 was introduced in 1979 to help DAF compete in the lucrative 8x4 dump truck market in the UK. It combined the best designs from both UK and Dutch engineers.

YA4440 – part of the Dutch military order for 4- and 5-ton equipment carriers.

In 1979, DAF finally joined the growing number of European truckmakers that had launched 8x4 chassis to compete against home-grown products in the British construction industry. The 2300 FAD was jointly developed by DAF's engineering teams in Holland and the UK, and featured a drivetrain of perfectly matched units. A novel feature of the truck was the use of crossmember technology to provide torsional rigidity, which negated the need for rear shock absorbers – a component that usually had a hard life on construction trucks.

As the decade drew to a close, DAF announced that production of trailers would cease, although special order trailers for the military would still be manufactured. By 1979 DAF had increased production to more than 15,000 vehicles a year, and the company was set to enter the next decade in excellent shape.

# The 1980s – one partner leaves and another joins

1980 heralded the introduction of the second generation 2800 series, together with a programme extension with twin-steer 6x2 and 8x4 models. This was followed by the introduction of special concrete mixer models, the 6x4 FMT 2300 and the more powerful 8x4 FND 2800.

There was also an up-to-date bonneted version, dubbed the N2800, which was a new 6x4 chassis designed to replace the DAF-engined International Paystar. This new model was designed as an on/off-road tipper chassis, intended primarily for export markets such as Africa and the Middle East. However, while the N-series had limited success in these markets, it did achieve notoriety by being used as a rally and support vehicle for the 1982 Paris-Dakar rally, actually winning first place for vehicles over 10 tons GVW.

In 1982 DAF introduced the F3300 series, which was intended for long distance transport and extra-heavy duty hauling. Powered by the DKX version of the 1160 engine, delivering some 330bhp, the F3300 became the premium alternative to the volume-selling 2800, which remained in production with 260bhp and 280bhp 1160 series powerplants.

The DKSE 'Economy' engine produced 280bhp at just

1980 saw the introduction of the second-generation of the F2800 series. (Courtesy DAF Trucks Ltd)

1800rpm, while the lower-powered version of the F2800, which used the 1160 DKTD engine, was to be the last big truck, low-power vehicle produced by DAF. Its place in the market was soon to be overtaken by the demand for small truck, high-power specifications, which ultimately produced better fuel efficiency and increased payload capacity.

The F3300 was introduced in 1982 and was designed for long-haul and extra heavy duty operations. It was powered by the 330bhp DKX engine. (Courtesy Niels Jansen)

This bonneted N-series 6x4 was intended to replace the ill-fated Paystar. Although designed for operation as an on/off-road dump truck, this particular example now operates as a recovery truck for a bus company in Moscow. (Courtesy Max Chern)

The F3300 was followed into production by upgrades to the smaller F218 cabbed trucks and tractors. The lightweight F2100 series was launched with the 210bhp version of the 8.25-litre diesel, and this was complemented by a new F2300, as well as the F2500 featuring a second-generation 8.25-litre diesel producing 250bhp. It was this new family of relatively high-powered lightweight trucks and tractors that replaced the 260bhp F2800 series.

With new products and upgrades flowing out of Eindhoven on a regular basis, DAF entered the 1980s in high spirits – but behind the scenes, its partnership with International Harvester was not working out as planned. Whilst DAF had enjoyed the financial input from IH's original 33 per cent share purchase, (which was increased to 37.5 per cent in 1980), the deal had never brought about a successful formula for the sharing of technology, designs, and, most importantly, markets.

One of the strangest DAFs was the MAG3300, custom-built especially for the air cargo industry. To ensure maximum body capacity the engine and cab were as far forward as possible, meaning twin radiators had to be installed ahead of the front wheels, but behind the cab steps. It is believed that a number of variations of the maximum capacity body theme were explored by DAF, including versions based on the integral bus chassis, and there were even versions built in conjunction with specialist truck builder GINAF. (Courtesy Niels Jansen)

Poor currency exchange rates and major differences between US and European truck designs, specifications, customer needs and expectations had effectively killed off any hopes of DAFs being sold in the US. In addition, with IH having already bought into rival truckmakers Seddon-Atkinson in England and Enasa in Spain, its resources were spread very thin and it was getting short of cash. So, International Harvester pulled out of DAF in 1983, and its shares were acquired by the VADO Group and DSM.

Another problem facing DAF was that by 1984 the F241 cab, as used on the 2800/3300 series, was ten years old, and sales had started to slow down. DAF marketeers across Europe knew that the New Truck Generation (NTG) team was working on a replacement for the F241 (which would ultimately become the 95 series), but also that it would not be available until 1988 at the very earliest.

So, with no face-lift or changes to the current model planned, DAF marketeers were keen to find some new angle that would help steady the flow of sales. As a result, the Present Truck Generation (PTG team), which was responsible for the 2800/3300 series, came up with a contingency plan divided into two stages: PTG 1 and PTG 2. In response to

3300 FAD 8x4 tipper. (Courtesy Richard Stanier)

In response to requests for a larger and more luxurious cab, DAF introduced the 3300 space cab.

enquiries from France for a larger and more luxurious cab to compete with the Volvo Globetrotter, DAF introduced the space cab with a high roof and improved driver comfort under PTG 1.

Eindhoven engineers kept the best until last, and under PTG 2 they revealed that development of more refined and yet more powerful 1160 series engines, destined for the NTG, was so far advanced that the new engines could be made available in the 2800/3300 series. In addition, a new range-topping 1160 DKZ, which used advanced turbocharging and intercooling to produce 373bhp SAE, would also allow the creation of the new 3600 series.

However, DAF's European marketeers had the problem of how to sell a great new engine in a truck that was indistinguishable from previous models. Peter Symons, who was DAF's UK product marketing manager at the time,

The ATI badging on the F3600, introduced in 1985, proved that having the correct badge could help improve sales of what was by then a ten-year-old design. (Courtesy Niels Jansen collection)

took part in a senior management meeting at Amsterdam's Schipol airport on Easter Friday 1985, and recalls Hans Staals explaining to the group that the new engine used advanced technology that was like second generation intercooling. This was to have a profound effect on Symons.

It was a decade when everybody was into labels, and having the right badge made a profound statement about both the product and its owner. So, back in England that weekend,

Peter mused over the current obsession with badges like GTI and XR3i on hot hatchbacks, and realised the answer lay in the right numeric badging for the 3600. Recalling Hans Staals' mention of second generation turbocharging, Peter came up with the idea of labelling the F3600 as having 'Advanced Turbo Intercooling', or ATI, and was pleasantly surprised when senior management at Eindhoven endorsed the suggestion. And the rest is history.

However, DAF's seasoned UK sales force were more than a little sceptical about the new branding. Former fleet sales manager Peter Jackson recalls: "When Peter Symons first presented the ATI concept to the UK salesforce we openly poured scorn on it. Boy were we wrong, however, as it produced high levels of both brand and product awareness, and even today hard core trucking types will recall the ATI badging with fondness."

Despite sales of its heavyweight trucks slowing down, September 1984 saw the 250,000th truck roll off the Eindhoven production line, and it was around this time that the NTG signed the CABTEC co-operation agreement

DAF 2500 tanker with non-standard wheels. (Courtesy Bill Clowes)

with ENASA-owned Pegaso in Spain, to jointly develop and manufacture a new high-tech cab for long-haul work. This would ultimately appear on the 95 series in 1987.

Early in 1986 DAF started an intensive co-operation programme with British Leyland, which resulted in the supply of DAF 8.25-litre DHTD engines for Leyland to install in the Leyland Constructor. More importantly, though, was the supply of lightweight Leyland-built distribution vehicles being badged as DAFs for sale in mainland Europe. Known within the company as DAF Distribution Vehicles, or DDVs, the first were the 600, 800 and 1000 series trucks, based on the Leyland Roadrunner, which would later become the 45 series.

These new small trucks effectively replaced the 'Club of Four'-developed ETD 500, 700 and 900 series trucks, and the deal was brokered directly between Eindhoven and Leyland without any involvement of DAF's management team in the UK, much to its consternation. Lightweight DAF trucks had never been available in the UK, and it seemed that these new successors to the ETD vehicles would also be destined for sale in Europe only. However, things were to change within a matter of months.

In late Autumn of 1986 Roger Phillips, the then managing director of DAF UK, held a secret meeting with George Simpson, the managing director of Leyland Trucks, together with senior sales and marketing personnel from both organisations, to discuss a possible amalgamation of the two companies. Leyland was in serious financial trouble, and the idea of a 'marriage' of the two manufacturers seemed to have some merit, so discussions were held to examine market forecasts for the next five years and identify which products from each range would be the best fit for each market.

In general, it was decided that if the companies were indeed to merge, DAF would concentrate on building tractors whilst Leyland would concentrate primarily on building rigids, although there were some exceptions, which will be explained later. Working groups appointed by both firms were tasked with refining the strategy to bring the amalgamation closer, and in January 1987 a meeting

was held at Amsterdam's Schipol airport. DAF's senior management revealed that it liked the UK product plan being put forward, and that both DAF UK and Leyland should now look at how each could rationalise its existing dealer network into a single entity.

Although several overseas companies were rumoured to be looking into acquiring Leyland at the time it was in discussion with DAF, the companies finally merged in April 1987, forming a new entity known as Leyland-DAF. Freight-Rover vans were also included in the new organisation, which now came under the control of a totally new company, DAF BV, with the Dutch holding the majority stake and exercising day-to-day control.

The truck operation of Leyland had already been drastically rationalised by early 1987, and under the terms of the deal with DAF the truck division was separated from the Leyland bus division, which in turn was the subject of a management buy-out. However, this latter entity operated as an independent for only a short period before it was sold to Volvo, which integrated Leyland bus models into its range before gradually replacing them with new Volvo models as they aged.

Whilst the merger with Leyland did not effect the DAF range in Europe – particularly as the lightweight Leyland-built DDV vehicles had already been launched on the continent a year earlier – it was a big issue in the UK. Although the new 'amalgamated' product range for the UK had been decided, research commissioned by DAF revealed that DAF-only branding would readily gain market acceptance. However, strong resistance from Leyland meant that did not happen for more than ten years.

It is estimated that DAF had approximately eight per cent of the UK truck market at the time of the merger, whilst Leyland had some 17 percent. The new entity had a management and culture driven by DAF, but with the volumes of Leyland. In addition to the formation of a new management structure for Leyland-DAF, and the rationalising of combined UK dealers down from 66 to 50 for the new brand, construction was already well under way on a brand new DAF UK headquarters building at Thame,

# New UK model configurations at formation of Leyland-DAF

| Previous model designation | New model designation |
|---|---|
| Leyland Roadrunner – 7.5-12 tons | Leyland-DAF 45 series |
| Leyland (lightweight) Freighter – 15-18 tons | Leyland-DAF 50 series |
| Leyland Freighter – 18 tons | Leyland-DAF 60 series |
| Leyland Constructor 6-26 tons[1] | Leyland-DAF 70 series |
| Leyland Constructor 8-32 tons[2] | Leyland-DAF 80 series |
| Leyland Roadtrain (low datum) – 48 tons | Leyland-DAF 80 series |
| DAF 2300/2700 – 32-ton tractor | Leyland-DAF 2300/2700 series[3] |
| DAF 2800/3300/3600 series | Leyland-DAF 95 series[4] |

[1] DAF 2300 FAT 6x4 discontinued in favour of Leyland-DAF 80 series 6x4
[2] DAF 2700 FAD 8X4 discontinued in favour of Leyland-DAF 80 series 8x4
[3] Leyland Cruiser discontinued in favour of Leyland-DAF 2300/2700 series
[4] Leyland Roadtrain (high datum) discontinued in favour of Leyland-DAF 95 series

The long-awaited 95 series was launched in 1987 under the Leyland-DAF brand in the UK, and as a DAF in other European markets. It was a superb new truck, voted European Truck of the Year in 1988. (Courtesy DAF Trucks Ltd)

in Oxfordshire, so the location for the management of the new organisation was easily decided.

The previous DAF UK HQ in Marlow was closed in October 1987, signalling the full integration of Leyland into DAF. The opening of the new DAF UK headquarters was a glitzy affair. Leyland-DAF could boast a brand new operating centre, but more importantly, the opening was timed to perfection to coincide with the launch of its new flagship truck range, the 95 series. This ultra-modern long-haul tractor, which was badged as Leyland-DAF in the UK and DAF elsewhere, featured the Cabtec tilt cab designed in conjunction with ENASA in Spain, and powered by 11.6-litre ATI engines developing 306, 352 or 383bhp, depending on specification.

The new truck was originally to be badged as the 120 in reference to the engine size (almost 12 litres), but fearing this was ultimately too unwieldy it was planned to change the numeral to 90. However, shortly before the new DAF's

Heavy haulage specialist Allelys was one of the very first operators to take delivery of a 380bhp 95 FTD 8x4 tractor, rated at 150 tons GTW. It's seen here offloading the Flying Scotsman steam locomotive. (Courtesy DAF Trucks Ltd)

launch the German truck manufacturer MAN unveiled its own new 90 series, so DAF was forced to make an eleventh hour switch to 95.

Approximately 250 customers, dealers, press and other VIPs flocked to the UK launch event at Thame every day for two weeks, whilst similar events were held across Europe for the launch of the identical DAF 95. Early examples of the 95 suffered teething problems, which some operators were quick to blame Leyland for, despite the fact that the new truck was 100 per cent DAF and built entirely in Eindhoven. However, this didn't stop the 95 series being voted European Truck of the Year twelve months after its launch.

# The 1990s – end of an era

DAF entered the 1990s in apprehensive mood. Whilst its new 95 series had been voted European Truck of the Year at the end of the 1980s, early teething troubles, problems encountered with former UK Leyland dealers now servicing DAF products, and a global recession combined to produce a dramatic slow-down in truck sales.

In addition to announcing face-lifted versions of the 1700, 1900 and 2300 series, together with the launch of the 2700 ATI to replace the 2500 series, DAF also introduced some basic models in an effort to boost ailing sales.

In the UK, the Leyland-DAF 80 series was a warmed-over, low datum Leyland Roadtrain fitted with the DAF ATI 330bhp engine, whilst the old F2800/3300 series, which had been phased out with the introduction of the 95 in 1987, was resurrected in 1991 as the 'basic' 2900/3200 series tractor. Aimed primarily at the Eastern European market, these were 'no frills' trucks built without modern electronics for simpler maintenance. They were relatively short-lived, and only small numbers were sold, but they

The 2700 ATI replaced the medium weight 2500 range. (Courtesy DAF Trucks Ltd)

underlined DAF's efforts to try and beat the recession by any means available.

At the same time as DAF announced an updated engine programme for 330bhp and 365bhp engines in the 95 series, as well as the introduction of a new 400bhp version, it also

46

In the UK the Leyland Roadtrain was fitted with the DAF 330bhp ATI engine and badged as the Leyland-DAF 80 series. It sold alongside the flagship 95 series as a low datum option. (Courtesy DAF Trucks Ltd)

The Leyland-DAF 80 series was relatively short-lived compared with the 95 series. (Courtesy DAF Trucks Ltd)

The old-style F2800-3600 series was resurrected, albeit briefly, in 1991 as the 2900/3200 series. It was intended as a low-tech, no-frills option for Eastern European markets. Like the Leyland-DAF 80 series, it was relatively short-lived. (Courtesy Richard Stanier)

became the first manufacturer to introduce a complete range of 9 NOx compliant engines. 1990 also witnessed the announcement of a joint-development programme with Renault for a new generation of vans, and also the separating of DAF Bus from the parent company to become part of United Bus.

In 1991, the previous 600, 800 and 1000 series – DAF versions of the Leyland-built Roadrunner light truck – were replaced by the DAF 45 series, a new generation of lightweight distribution trucks featuring the 5.88-litre Cummins engine, with a strong heritage from the Leyland Roadrunner.

The 400bhp version of the 95 became available in 1991. (Courtesy DAF Trucks Ltd)

A 330bhp diesel powers this 95 series drawbar outfit operated by Eddie Stobart. (Courtesy DAF Trucks Ltd)

Second generation 75 and 85 series were introduced in 1992. (Courtesy DAF Trucks Ltd)

Not known as a company that rested on its laurels, the following year witnessed the arrival of the second generation 95 series for long-haul duties, which was equipped with a 9 NOx compliant WS ATI engine, supplemented with a 428bhp version.

At the Hanover Show in 1992, DAF announced further second generation models, this time for 75 and 85 series for medium and heavyweight distribution operations, as well as for utility transports. Additionally, the 45 series was now available with a sleeper cab, and DAF was also able to introduce its first Euro 1 compliant 8 NOx engine.

1993 was a disastrous year for DAF as the global recession, which had been building since 1989, impacted heavily on the UK commercial vehicle market where sales plummeted to levels not seen since wartime. As the UK was DAF's largest market, repercussions were inevitable, as were the consequences of a severe downturn in the continental European markets in 1992.

Despite efforts to save the company, on 2nd February 1993 the receivers were called in and it was declared bankrupt. Fortunately, within a month the Dutch and Belgian governments, both having a vested interest in safeguarding local jobs, decided to bail out the company. So, on 2nd March 1993 a new company, DAF Trucks NV, was formed.

The UK manufacturing operation of the old Leyland-DAF business was not part of the new deal, and for a while it looked like the Lancashire-based company would close its doors for good. However, a management buyout at Leyland in June 1993 proved the salvation of truck-building in the town. So Leyland became separate from DAF once again. However, the new firm of Leyland Truck Manufacturing signed an agreement with DAF to build and supply trucks to be sold under the DAF name.

In September that same year DAF

1994 was a good year for the 85 series, which was voted Fleet Truck of the Year. (Courtesy DAF Trucks Ltd)

announced its first Euro 2 compliant ATI engine, and so became the first European manufacturer to supply engines with a noxious gas emission level reduced to 7 NOx. This was more than two years ahead of the mandatory introduction date of October 1996.

However, in addition to the quest for more environmentally-friendly engines, there was also a burgeoning desire for increased power beyond that available from the 428bhp ATI engine. So, in January 1994 DAF dropped a proprietary engine in the shape of a 507bhp Cummins into the 95 series, and launched the 95.500 model, which also featured a newly developed super space cab – the largest sleeper cab available for long-haul at that time. The new super-power 95 wasn't a volume seller, but it did help the 95 series reach a production output of 50,000 units by 30th November that year.

1994 was also a good year for the 85 series, which was voted UK Fleet Truck of the Year, and towards the end of the year was destined for export throughout North Africa and the Middle East after a factory for its local assembly was set up in Casablanca, Morocco. A year later, it was announced that the 85 series would be assembled in China by the Chanfeng Auto Corp, and in 1996, a new DAF subsidiary was launched in Warsaw, Poland.

However, the really big news came on 15th November 1996, when DAF became part of US-based PACCAR Inc, the parent company of Kenworth, Peterbilt and Foden. At a stroke, DAF was now part of the world's largest truck manufacturing group, and one that was pre-eminent in most of the world's truck markets.

Unlike other takeovers and amalgamations, which usually led to the demise of one or more brands within a

The trendsetting 95XF was introduced in 1997, with power outputs of up to 530bhp. It was easily distinguished from the previous 95 series by the 'mouth' below the slatted grille. It was voted International Truck of the Year for 1998. (Courtesy Bill Clowes)

large group, PACCAR had no intention of interfering with the DAF brand or product range. Instead, it actively encouraged innovation and brand autonomy. Subsequently, DAF kicked off 1997 with the introduction of the trendsetting 95XF, designed specifically for long-haul work, in both 4x2 and 6x2 variants complete with comfort cab, space cab, and super space cab options.

The company also used this model to launch its newly developed 12.6-litre, six in-line 24 valve diesel engine with power outputs of between 381 and 530bhp. The 95XF proved to be the perfect truck for heavyweight and long-distance haulage and an international panel of journalists agreed, voting it the International Truck of the Year for 1998.

Having operated as an independent UK manufacturing contractor to DAF since its management buyout in 1993, Leyland Truck Manufacturing was acquired by PACCAR in 1998, finally bringing both DAF and Leyland back under the same umbrella.

This 95XF is seen here hauling a B-train double trailer combination in New Zealand. (Courtesy Rod Simmonds)

Following the launch of the super space cab, DAF introduced special 'super space cab weekends' at the Eindhoven factory. These popular events were attended by truck operators from across Europe. (Courtesy DAF Trucks NV)

# 21st century trucks – preparing for the future

Taking into account everything that had happened to DAF, including bankruptcy, assorted partners, mergers and owners, as well as manufacturing everything from cars and trailers to vans, trucks and buses, before divesting itself of everything that was non-core to truck building, one could quite rightly view the first 50 years or so of the company as preparation for the future. And it was a bright future indeed that DAF trucks looked towards, as it entered a brand new millennium with the global muscle of PACCAR supporting it.

Its flagship 95XF, launched three years earlier, had already been crowned International Truck of the Year, followed up by production of the 500,000th truck to roll off the Eindhoven lines since truck building first began. However, January 1st 2000 also witnessed another minor landmark: it heralded the demise of the Leyland-DAF brand in the UK.

Apart from the Leyland-built lightweight 45 series, all of the old Leyland-designed trucks had been phased out by 1993, and with market intelligence indicating that UK dealers and operators had a preference for the DAF name, there was no better time to consign the old Leyland-DAF branding to the history books.

DAF was exceedingly well prepared for the new millennium, with its range-topping 95XF just a couple of years old, and a fresh mid-range CF series developed from the 75/85 series. However, in order to ensure that its product line-up was the most modern and technically advanced in the industry, it launched the upgraded 'new' CF in 2001, and followed this with the lightweight LF – a worthy successor to the 45 series.

## DAF LF

With a heritage that can be traced back through the Leyland-built DAF 45 to Leyland's original lightweight creation, the Roadrunner, the DAF LF series (unofficially standing for Light Forte) was designed exclusively for the distribution industry. It was, and still is, the most stylish of trucks in the 7.5- to 18-ton sector, taking the European delivery truck market by storm.

Introduced at the Brussels Motor Show in 2001, the LF45 and LF55 series replaced the previous DAF 45/55 models, providing high operating efficiencies and driver comfort combined with low weight and low operating costs. This excellent mix of benefits was not lost on the international transport judges, who elected the LF International Truck of the Year for 2002.

Brand new, from one end to the other, the LF shared a basic cab structure with Renault and used four- and six-cylinder PACCAR engines, developed in conjunction with Cummins. At its launch, the 3.9-litre, four-cylinder diesel could be specified in three power outputs from 135bhp to 167bhp, whilst the six-cylinder, 5.9-litre engine could be specified with outputs from 185bhp to 250bhp. Five- and six-speed ZF gearboxes were available, together with an Eaton nine-speeder and fully-automatic Allison transmission for special applications.

Further into production, engine displacement of the four-cylinder diesel increased to 4.5 litres, whilst the six-cylinder engine grew to 6.7 litres. This increased power ratings to between 140bhp and 285bhp, all meeting Euro 4 and Euro 5 emissions standards. At the same time, the automated six-speed AS-Tronic gearbox became an option throughout the range.

The heritage of DAF's LF series can be traced back to the Leyland Roadrunner 7.5-tonner, which latterly became the

Leyland-DAF 45 series. (Courtesy DAF Trucks Ltd)

Whilst the LF increased in popularity across Europe, there was also a growing awareness amongst truck operators of their carbon footprint, with many operators electing to 'go green' to demonstrate their contribution to reducing emission levels. So, in 2006 DAF launched the updated LF and CF series with a completely new programme of PACCAR engines with SCR technology for Euro 4 and Euro 5 emissions standards.

At the IAA Hanover Show in September that year, DAF presented a prototype hybrid truck based on the LF. The vehicle had a diesel/electric hybrid system, whereby the truck could be driven by the diesel engine, the electric motor, or a combination of both, resulting in a significant reduction of fuel consumption and emissions. Then in 2007 DAF commenced production of extra-clean EEV engines. By applying a soot filter to engines meeting Euro 5 emission standards, a further 50 per cent reduction in the emission of soot particles was achieved, and emission levels were reached that were only thought possible with gas engines.

The EEV – Enhanced Environmentally-friendly Vehicle – was mandated in 1999 by EC Directive 1999/96/EC as a standard for natural gas engine emissions, particularly for public transport. It was never expected that diesel engines would achieve these levels, but such was the progress made by DAF SCR technology that DAF's new EEV-compliant

57

The versatility of the DAF LF55-220 is demonstrated by this 18-ton GVW dropside.
(Courtesy Ryder Ltd)

The DAF LF 55 has become the delivery truck of choice for a wide variety of breweries.
(Courtesy Ryder Ltd)

LF45-160 EEV. (Courtesy Ryder Ltd)

engines produced lower emissions than most natural gas-powered units.

When the LF45 7.5-tonner with the EEV-compliant FR160bhp engine was made available for road testing, leading UK transport publications Motor Transport and Commercial Motor both achieved a fuel consumption of 21.5mpg, whilst Transport News in Scotland achieved 20.85mpg. This was above the magical 20mpg figure on every sector of the test course.

However, not being a company to rest on its laurels, DAF further improved the LF in the summer of 2009 with a host of new features, including chassis modifications, a revised interior, and Euro 5 high-output engines. At this time, both the 4.5-litre PACCAR FR four-cylinder 210bhp unit and the 6.7-litre 300bhp PACCAR GR six-cylinder engine received increased injector pressure and a revised engine management system, along with redesigned pistons.

LFs are available in both rigid and tractor form, with either day or sleeper cab options. LF45s range from 7.5 to 12 tons, whilst the LF55s stretch from 13 to 21 tons gross vehicle weight and can accommodate gross train weights of 32 tons.

## DAF CF

The DAF CF was developed and refined from the 65/75/85 series, which was first launched at the Hanover Show in April 1992. Designed primarily for medium and heavyweight distribution operations, as well as for utility transports, the 'Compact Forte' trucks quickly developed into a full range of two, three and four-axle trucks and tractors.

The 'upgraded' CF was launched in 2001, with the top specification CF85 series featuring DAF-designed PACCAR MX engines up to 510bhp in the CF85, while the CF75 was equipped with the revised 9.2-litre PACCAR PR engine ranging from 250bhp to 360bhp. Making up the CF trio, the versatile 65 series featured the 6.7-litre GR engine with power outputs between 220bhp and 285bhp. All of them came equipped with DAF SCR technology.

Over the years the DAF CF has proven to be a most versatile and popular truck, and in the summer of 2009 it emerged victorious in a five-way fight for the

This CF 85-460 drawbar outfit can operate at up to 50 tons GVW in Holland. (Courtesy DAF Trucks NV)

The CF 85-460 6x2 44-ton GVW tractor is the ideal workhorse for long-haul operators. (Courtesy Ryder Ltd)

The CF 8x4 FAD has proven to be an extremely popular truck in the European construction industry. (Courtesy DAF Trucks NV)

*Motor Transport* magazine Fleet Truck of the Year award. It was the second year in succession that the CF had claimed the title, and the sixth time in ten years that a DAF had won the award.

"The CF85 meets all of an operator's needs for reliability, back-up, cost management and driver satisfaction. By far the best overall vehicle." So concluded the jury after a comparison of five different vehicles in the final round for the award.

The CF 65-220 proved a popular choice for operators requiring a high quality, 18-ton truck.
(Courtesy Ryder Ltd)

25m three trailer CF rig from Holland.
(Courtesy Niels Jansen)

# DAF XF

In 2002 DAF completed its model upgrade programme with the successor to the 95XF – the XF95, featuring a slightly modified exterior, lighter chassis, disc brakes, and an optional AS-Tronic automatic gearbox. However, the XF95's reign as king of the DAF hill lasted just three years. At the end of 2005, low operating costs, best driver satisfaction and high reliability inspired the launch of the range-topping XF105.

At the same time, the DAF XE series engines rated at 430, 480 and 530bhp were replaced with the PACCAR 12.9-litre MX engine variants, rated at 410, 460 and 510bhp.

However, whilst maximum power marginally decreased, the real advantage was the dramatic increase in engine torque that now occurred at lower RPMs. For example, maximum torque went up from 1950 to 2000Nm (430XE-1900rpm to 410MX-1450rpm); 2100 to 2300Nm (480XE-1900rpm to 460MX-1450rpm); and 2350 to 2500Nm (530XE-1900rpm to 510MX-1450rpm), all delivering more power through the green band on the tacho. A 560bhp high torque MX engine was also in development, but the increasing environmental pressures saw the project put on ice until such an engine would be needed.

This 95XF was used to haul the Orange Arrows F1 team to European race circuits. (Courtesy DAF Trucks Ltd)

The XF95 replaced the 95XF in 2002, and although it had a similar shaped 'mouth' it was distinguishable by having sloping sides to the upper grille, and the previously square headlights were replaced by moulded twin headlights. (Courtesy DAF Trucks Ltd)

The XF105 was introduced in 2006 and can be visually distinguished from the XF95 by its deeper 'mouth' which extends well into the bumper, as well as the horizontal chrome trim at the top of the mouth. (Courtesy DAF Trucks NV)

Production of the XF105 commenced in 2006, with the PACCAR MX engines using SCR technology for either Euro 4 or 5 exhaust gas emission standard specifications. Mated to either a 16-speed manual or AS-Tronic automatic transmission with a standard hypoid rear axle, the big XF could also be specified with a hub-reduction axle for extra heavy duty applications.

Setting new standards in quality, efficiency and performance, the XF105 was named International Truck of the Year for 2007, and helped DAF set new records in truck production. By comparison, at the end of the 1980s, around 18,000 trucks were being produced annually at the

Eindhoven plant, and by the end of the 1990s this figure had risen to around 25,000 per annum. By 2004 this had risen to 31,000, and in 2006 the 40,000 barrier was broken.

However, in 2007, more than 42,500 medium and heavy duty trucks were produced at Eindhoven, whilst the PACCAR-owned Leyland Trucks plant in the UK built a further 11,500 LFs, plus more than 6000 UK-assembled CFs and XF105s, bringing the total annual production for both plants to a whopping 60,500 units. The same year, the 750,000th Eindhoven-built truck rolled off the production line, making DAF Europe's fastest growing truck manufacturer.

The following year saw the PACCAR-owned Leyland

XF105 6x4 with the 510bhp PACCAR MX engine. (Courtesy DAF Trucks Ltd)

Trucks plant in Lancashire complete assembly of the 300,000th truck to be produced at the plant, whilst for the fourteenth successive year DAF led the UK market with a 27.3 per cent share. It registered 13,290 new vehicles during 2008, and showed the largest yearly increase in sales of any other truck manufacturer – almost double those of its nearest UK competitor, Mercedes. In fact, for the fourth year running, DAF led in all eight sectors of the UK truck market – no other truck manufacturer had ever achieved for a single month.

In 2009 DAF received the ultimate accolade for the XF when it was voted Best Truck Ever in a survey of UK truck drivers by the magazine Truck & Driver. "It's perhaps fitting

These stunning XF105 6x2s with 410bhp are part of the fleet of Ramage Transport of Newcastle Upon Tyne. (Courtesy DAF Trucks Ltd)

that the winner of our poll is a truck currently in production," commented Will Shiers, editor of Truck & Driver. "While many old salts out there might get all misty eyed recalling their own favourites from days gone by, in truth these visions cannot hold a candle to the modern supertruck as epitomised by DAF's current XF flagship." The Scania 143 was voted into second place ahead of the Volvo F88 in third.

Today, as a wholly-owned subsidiary of PACCAR, DAF Trucks NV sees itself as a technology company and the premier commercial vehicle manufacture in Europe. It focuses exclusively on designing and building innovative and high-quality highway hauliers, having consigned the manufacture of trailers, buses and military vehicles largely to history, along with its involvement in motor sport.

XF105 6x2 with 460bhp. (Courtesy DAF Trucks Ltd)

This XF105 6x2 drawbar outfit operates at 25.5 metre overall length and up to a maximum of 60 tons GVW in Holland. (Courtesy Niels Jansen)

Everybody that I spoke to as part of my research for this book was very complimentary of PACCAR and the way that it has helped DAF become the tour de force it is today. In fact, the differences between the two organisations were aptly described by one ex-DAF employee: "DAF was a small family engineering business that became a large family engineering business, whereas PACCAR is an organisation run by business people that just happen to build trucks."

Today, DAF's engine factory, component plant, press shop and final assembly line for the CF and XF models are located in Eindhoven. Axles and cabs are produced in Westerlo, Belgium, whilst PACCAR-owned Leyland Trucks in the UK produces the entire range of LF light and medium weight trucks for all markets, as well as CF and XF105 vehicles specifically for the UK market.

In the spring of 2009, despite a slump in the sales of new trucks due to the global recession, the Leyland Trucks plant at Farington, Lancashire, received the Queen's Award for International Trade due to the plant's exceptional performance in building DAF trucks for global markets. Almost 40 per cent of the plant's output is shipped to 44 overseas markets, including Western and Eastern Europe, as well as such distant locations as South Africa, Australia and Mexico.

In summing up DAF's position in the truck market, some 60 years after the first trucks rolled off the Eindhoven Assembly lines, Rob Appels, DAF's head of corporate communications, states: "DAF is driven by the desire to deliver quality. We purposely get close to customers and drivers to produce vehicles that are not only built for the job, but add real value to customers' business. All DAFs are designed to the highest standards, and you won't see us introducing new technology just for the sake of it."

Those that would like to glance backwards to reflect on what DAF achieved in the 20th century would do well to visit DAF's birthplace, which has now been turned into the DAF Museum in the heart of Eindhoven. First opened in 1993, the museum features beautifully restored DAF cars, trucks and buses from every decade of manufacture, many of which are set in period street settings. There's everything from trailers, military vehicles, race trucks and engines on display alongside a wide range of trucks, and if you are lucky, you may even see the latest addition undergoing a total restoration.

This FX105 is operated by Edinburgh-based crane hire and machinery movement expert, Bernard Hunter.
(Courtesy DAF Trucks Ltd)

# People carriers

### Buses

Whilst this book is primarily dedicated to the history and development of DAF as a truck builder, the story of the Eindhoven-based manufacturer would be incomplete without at least a passing glance at some of the company's other notable achievements in the arena of passenger carrying and lightweight freight vehicles.

In post-war Holland there was an urgent need to rebuild, and large numbers of workers were required for the task. With much of the passenger transport system in a damaged condition, DAF was asked to build 300 passenger-carrying semi-trailers, largely for the Dutch State Railways. Although these trailers were later banned under Dutch traffic law, they carried millions of Dutch men and women to work each day, and played a major role in getting Holland's trade and industry moving again.

Tractor units for the trailers consisted of a mix of ex-military Dodges and Chevrolets, with large numbers of Seddons and Crossleys imported from Britain also. While bus and truck chassis started rolling off the Eindhoven production line in 1949, DAF's first motorised passenger carrying vehicles were a batch of prototype, single-deck electric trolleybuses, production of which commenced as early as

One of a batch of DAF trolleybuses built for the city of Groningen.
(Courtesy Hans Houtsma)

1947. Constructed in conjunction with Dutch bodybuilder Verheul, eight were built and operated very successfully in the city of Groningen, in the north of Holland, until 1965.

At the first postwar motor show in Amsterdam, in 1948, DAF presented its motor bus chassis with an innovative slide-mounted engine. This allowed the whole assembly to move forward out of the front of the bus in a matter of seconds for routine maintenance or repairs.

Two DAF BD 52s. The 1951 coach nearest the camera has bodywork by Van Rooyen, whilst the 1954 behind has bodywork by Jongerius. (Courtesy Niels Jansen collection)

The first diesel-powered DAF bus and coach chassis was the truck-derived B-series, launched in 1953 and available in 1100, 1300 and 1600 designations for bodies carrying between 30-49 passengers. These proved particularly popular throughout Africa and South America, and they followed the conventional front engine layout.

Early chassis were powered by petrol engines from Waukesha and Hercules, with Perkins and Hercules diesel options. However, as a result of DAF developing and manufacturing its own refined version of the Leyland 0.350 diesel – which became the 120bhp DD575 – from 1957 onwards bus and chassis were only available with DAF-built diesel engines. These were followed in 1959 by the

introduction of the 'Tram Bus' TB 160 DD bus chassis, also powered by the 120bhp DD575 diesel. This had a set-back front axle that allowed front entrance bus and coach layouts, whilst retaining the conventional front engine configuration.

Aside from trucks, perhaps the second largest single vehicular project for DAF during the 1960s and 1970s was the development of the standard Dutch city bus. Bus chassis had always featured in the DAF product range and from the early 1960s mid-engined and rear-engined chassis, for both bus and coach work, had largely superceded the early front-engined layout. The latter now only being available for certain export markets.

DAF worked with leading Dutch coachbuilder Den Oudsten to design a standard city bus.

DAF also worked with Den Oudsten to produce a small batch of trolleybuses for Arnhem, which today operates the last remaining trolleybus system in Holland. (Courtesy Ferry Bosman)

The public transportation departments of Amsterdam, Rotterdam and The Hague undertook a study of their requirements for a standardised city bus. The cities were later joined by Utrecht and Groningen, and by using the 180bhp 11.1-litre rear-underfloor-engined DAF SB200 bus chassis as the basis, a hybrid body and chassis evolved, which used Voith automatic transmission and had standard bodywork, constructed largely by Dutch coachbuilder Hainje.

The project, designated SB201, resulted in the construction of almost 2000 virtually identical buses. This resulted in significant reductions in maintenance and servicing costs for the five cities, which helped considerably in containing the costs of public transport. In 1978 DAF redesigned its standardised city bus chassis, designating it the SB 210 DKL.

The late 1970s was also the period when DAF made its

first inroads into the UK bus and coach market, with a type of chassis not previously used in the country in significant numbers. At the time, the UK coach market was dominated by two rival coachbuilding firms, Duple and Plaxton, which largely used traditional straight chassis frames with underfloor engines, onto which bodies were mounted.

As Bedford and Ford bowed out of the lightweight bus chassis market, Leyland and Volvo bus chassis seemed to have the heavyweight market to themselves. However, DAF saw this as a great market opportunity and decided to enter the arena. As the outpourings of Belgian and Portuguese coachbuilders also began to appear in the UK, DAF took the decision to import its rear-engined SB2000 chassis and concentrate on the burgeoning integral coach market, which had been pioneered by Eindhoven-based coachbuilder BOVA in 1969 using DAF running gear.

Coachbuilders were beginning to focus on high-floor coaches, which provided increased luggage carrying capacity in underfloor lockers. The traditional centrally-mounted underfloor engine layout proved to be largely unsuitable for these new designs. However, the rear-engined DAF proved ideal for the task, and to supplement this the company conducted research into the natural frequency of chassis framework. As a result, DAF engineered a design that not only produced a level of integral body stiffness that could not be achieved with a conventional mid-engined layout, but also reduced vibrations, reduced weight, and allowed for an unparalleled level of ride smoothness.

Whilst other European chassis makers developed rear-engined designs of their own, DAF was unique in supplying front and rear drivetrain subframes coupled via a mobile jig. This jig allowed DAF to supply coachbuilders with a complete mobile 'structure' and guaranteed perfect alignment of bodywork to running gear.

Once the coachbuilder had assembled the basic bodyshell around the chassis, the central mobile jig could be cut out without fear of the vehicle's integrity or alignment being compromised. The UK bus and coach market had been married to the concept of body-on-chassis construction for decades, and so needed reassuring that this new concept

Locally bodied and assembled DAF bus in Morocco.
(Courtesy Max Chern)

was sound. However, as more and more integrals appeared on the market so acceptance of the benefits grew.

During the 1980s the bus market grew ever challenging for DAF, particularly in its home market of Holland. It was proving increasingly difficult, if not frustrating, to accommodate the constant and complex changes that bus operators throughout Holland wanted to incorporate into designs. Prior to 1983 DAF had something of a monopoly on home market city and intercity buses, but changes to government buying policies allowed bus operators freedom to purchase vehicles from any manufacturer.

The frustration of trying to accommodate the constant design changes required by Dutch bus operators meant that development of a standard DAF city bus was proving increasingly difficult to achieve. So, DAF switched its focus to export markets, selling a number of SB220s to Madrid after convincing the local DAF truck dealer to service them. Other notable export successes included Norway, Denmark, Greece and Morocco.

DAF DB250 double-decker in the UK, with bodywork by Northern Counties.

In 1988 a dedicated bus chassis assembly line was constructed at Eindhoven, and the company once again pushed ahead with its dream of a standard city bus design. However, knowing that Dutch bus operators would always find a flaw in any vehicle's design if they had not been allowed to add their own engineering thoughts to the design process, DAF decided to design and build prototypes in conjunction with local coachbuilder Den Oudsten, in total secrecy.

To overcome the 'not invented here' mindset of Dutch bus operators, the prototype DAF Alliance bus was exhibited as an 'export-only' vehicle, which certainly intrigued home market operators. So, not wishing to miss out on this radical new design they placed large orders.

In 1989, DAF Bus was finally separated from the core truck-building business and renamed DAF Bus International. A year later it joined forces with Eindhoven-based coachbuilder BOVA to form United Bus. It was later joined by Den Oudsten from Holland, Optare from the UK, and DAB from Denmark.

One of the first collaborations produced by United Bus was the 1991 launch of the DAF DB250 double-decker, which was initially sold using a variety of bus bodies, including those from Optare and Northern Counties in the UK. The original design was based on the MCW Metrobus, for which Optare and DAF Bus International brought the rights when MCW's parent company, the Laird Group, decided to sell off its bus and rail divisions in 1989.

DAF Bus International became a subsidiary of VDL Group after United Bus collapsed in 1993. The collaboration between DAF and Optare ultimately led to the introduction of the VDL DB250, which was sold in the UK through VDL's international dealer, Arriva Bus & Coach.

DAF engines are still used in many VDL buses and coaches today, with many retaining their original DAF SB designations. DAF's parent company, PACCAR, owns a 19 per cent stake in VDL, and was probably most pleased when DAF earned the accolade of Best Coach Engine Producer of the Year 2007 at the Bus World Asia event in Shanghai, as a result of the reliability and durability of the PACCAR 9.2-litre and 12.9-litre engines. The company followed this up by winning the award again in 2008 and 2009.

DAF Pony hauling a DAF 33 car. (Courtesy the DAF Museum)

## Cars

The van Doorne brothers had nurtured aspirations to create a Dutch car-building empire since the early postwar years, and at the 1958 RAI European Road Transport Show in Amsterdam they caused a sensation when they launched their first car, the DAF 600. It was powered by a twin-cylinder 590cc engine with a revolutionary, fully automatic CVT transmission called Variomatic. This innovative gearless design eliminated the need for a differential, with drivebelts taking up the difference of speed when cornering.

The first 600s rolled off the NedCar production line in the city of Born, southern Holland, a year later, soon followed by a 746cc version, aptly named the 750. DAF later produced a more luxurious version called the Daffodil, which had three numeric types: DAF30, 31 and 32. These were supplemented in 1966 by the larger type 44, with styling by Michelotti and a more powerful 850cc twin-cylinder engine.

In addition to powering the small cars, the 746cc, 30bhp SAE powerplant, complete with Variomatic transmission, was also used in a short-lived, small DAF van and truck known as the Pony. With a payload of 0.35 tons, and a gross weight of 1.1 tons, the Pony could average an impressive 35mpg around town.

In 1968 the company broke with tradition by introducing the DAF 55, which used the 1108cc water-cooled four-cylinder engine from the Renault 8. This was later replaced by the boxy type 66.

Volvo gained an interest in the small DAF cars early in the 1970s, as it was keen to introduce a small car range of its own. So, in 1974 the Swedish auto maker took over the Born plant and quietly dropped the 33 and 44 models, and re-badged the DAF 66 as the Volvo 66. Interestingly, the last DAF prototype – the DAF 77 – became the Volvo 343, which sold almost 1.3m units.

# Military hardware

One of the longest running chapters in the history of DAF is its involvement in the production of military vehicles. The manufacture of everything from trailers, multi-wheel drive systems and lightweight 4x4s through to armoured cars, 6x6 trucks and even tank transporters has seen the Eindhoven truck builder develop an enviable reputation for military hardware spanning more than 70 years.

The wartime period is covered in detail in chapter 1, however in the immediate postwar years, the van Doornes returned to producing the core products that they had become famous for – semi-trailers and drawbar trailers – but the concept of becoming a fully-fledged automaker was never far from their minds. One of DAF's most notable projects during this time was the building of several types of

aircraft refuelling units and a special fast refuelling trailer, some of which were ordered by the US airforce stationed in Holland.

The very first DAF trucks, introduced at the end of 1949, were lightweight A-30 models produced at the old trailer works for the Dutch army. However, following the formation of NATO, the Dutch government offered DAF the contract for production of a new all-wheel-drive military vehicle. Normally DAF would have jumped at such an offer, but its factory was already operating at its limits. A new facility would be needed.

The result was a huge new factory (60,000 square metres of floor space). Much of the funding came from the USA and its newly set-up Marshall Aid Plan, implemented

DAF developed two YA 054 prototypes in 1951, as possible replacements for ageing wartime jeeps being used by the Royal Dutch army. (Courtesy the DAF Museum)

YA 328 undergoing testing in 1952. (Courtesy the DAF Museum)

In 1951, just after the Willys M38A1 went into production in the US, DAF attempted to develop its own 1/4-ton 4x4 vehicle. DAF pinned its hopes on this new vehicle being the front-running candidate to replace the old Willys and Ford jeeps being used by the Royal Dutch army at the time, and two prototypes of the proposed YA 054 were produced.

The vehicle was 355cm (140in) in overall length, slightly longer than the M38A1, and had a longer wheelbase at 220cm (86.5 inches). Powered by a Hercules four-cylinder petrol engine, the YA 054 weighed 1600kg (3200 pounds) with a 500kg (1100 pound) payload, similar to the ubiquitous Jeep.

The DAF light-terrain vehicle had the H drivetrain, which was developed for the YA 318 and YA 328 3-ton trucks. The system used in YA 054 consisted of a central differential connected to two distribution boxes located at the sides of the vehicle. These distribution boxes were connected to front and rear wheels by means of four small driveshafts along the sides. Drive to the rear wheels could be manually disconnected for road conditions where two-wheel drive was adequate.

Without the need for large central driveshafts, ground clearance was good, and with a three-speed gear box and high and low-range transfer case, the vehicle performed well on rough terrain. Ultimately, the Royal Dutch army elected to buy the Willys M38A1 because the YA 054 had apparently never been approved by NATO. So, without the support of its own country's military, DAF did not move the project beyond the prototype stage. It could also be argued that with hundreds of YA 328s and YA 126s being churned out alongside civilian trucks there would not have been the capacity to build the YA 054 anyway, which is a shame.

During the period of the Marshall Plan some $13

manufacturer, and laid firm foundations for its continued success.

One of these vehicles was the DAF YA 314 4x4 truck, which had a payload of 3000kg. Developed during the early 1950s, the truck was eventually put into production in 1953 and was manufactured right up to 1965. It was built with a basic steel forward control cab with a canvas roof that could be rolled backwards, whilst the windscreen could be folded forward on to the radiator if required. It also had removable doors. A development of this truck, the YA 414, was eventually built under licence in Spain by Enasa, and sold as the Pegaso 3045D.

Another DAF 4x4 army vehicle developed around the same time was the YA 126, which was a lightweight bonneted truck fitted with an in-line, six-cylinder Hercules 4.6-litre petrol engine. Designed primarily for use as a weapons carrier, radio truck or ambulance/fire tender, it had a frontal appearance not dissimilar to the ill-fated YA 054 jeep clone.

Such was the predominance of military vehicle production around the mid-1950s that a number of major milestones were almost overlooked. Not only was the 10,000th civilian truck chassis completed in May 1955, but October of that year also saw the delivery of the 5000th military vehicle to the Dutch army.

There was another revival of military activity in the late 1960s, when DAF received a contract from the Dutch army to build an advanced personnel carrier. The company's solution was the YP 408, a high performance 8x6 machine that could be adapted to a variety of roles. These included duties as troop carriers, ambulances and armoured patrol vehicles, as well as being used as field artillery tractors or mobile command posts. Several hundred were built between 1963 and 1969 with virtually all of them still

The prototype FTT 3500 tank transporter may have used the cab from the 2600, but all similarities with that series ended there. Lurking in the frame of this monster was a 13.95-litre 475bhp V12 Detroit Diesel motor. Sadly, this time around DAF didn't win the contract from the Dutch army, which went instead to rival FTF (Floor Trailer Factory of Nijmegen), which also installed the same Detroit Diesel motor. (Courtesy the DAF Museum)

Some 6500 YA 4440 four-tonners were built by DAF for the Dutch army in the late 1970s and early 1980s. They saw many years of service, and were eventually replaced by the YA 4442. (Courtesy the DAF Museum)

In 1975, DAF submitted a tender to the quartermaster general's department of the Netherlands armed forces for the supply of a 4x4 four-tonner, designated the type YA 4440. A year later it received an order for 4000 trucks. These new generation vehicles were designed to replace the ageing YA 314 and YA 328 trucks that had been supplied to the Dutch army in the 1950s. The first of the YA 4440s were delivered in 1978, and production ran until 1982 alongside a repeat order for a further 2500 four-tonners.

At the height of the Cold War in the 1980s, the British ministry of defence (MoD) was also looking for a new four ton general cargo truck to replace its ageing fleet of Bedfords. Tenders were sought for an initial batch of 5000 trucks, with a possible repeat order for a further 5000. AWD – which had by then taken over the assembly of the former Bedford range – and Volvo were invited to tender alongside the new Leyland-DAF consortium.

The MoD was keen to avoid acquiring a fleet of

Leyland-DAF in the UK built large numbers of 4x4 four-tonners for the British army based on the Leyland Roadrunner truck. In addition, Watford-based Scammell Motors (also part of Leyland-DAF) constructed a number of S26 8x6 trucks that were specifically designed for the army's Demountable Rack Off-loading Pallet System (DROPS). (Courtesy DAF Trucks Ltd)

'military specials' and instead take full advantage of the premium truck technology that was becoming the norm for commercial fleet owners. Therefore, by looking to acquire vehicles with standard off-the-shelf components, the cost of servicing and replacement parts could be minimised.

The contract was eventually awarded to the Leyland-DAF plant in the UK, and the ultimate design specifications drew heavily on vehicle trials conducted in harsh operating conditions on African roads. Recognising that the vehicles would still be in service well into the 21st century,

Leyland-DAF came up with a vehicle specification that was forward-looking and included permanent four-wheel-drive and a high datum cab, although the specification of this highlighted one of the many problems associated with military contracts.

Peter Jackson recalls: "A number of the trucks were specified with an opening cab roof hatch and machine gun mount, so we assumed that there was a standard design and set of specifications for this. But when we asked for an example to copy, we were somewhat flabbergasted when we were directed to the Imperial War Museum in London."

Whilst DAF concentrated primarily on building civilian trucks during the 1990s, more recently it has constructed a number of specialist heavy transporters for the Dutch army, and acknowledges at the time of writing that it is still active in the production of military vehicles.

In 2002, the Royal Netherlands army placed an order with DAF for a batch of 39 heavy equipment/tank transporter vehicles with a 65-ton payload capacity, 63 heavy equipment transporters with a 40-ton payload capacity, and ten spare tractor units. The vehicles are known as the TROPCO system, which is an abbreviation of trekkeropleggercombinatie (or tractor/semi-trailer combination).

To fulfil the contract, DAF teamed up with Dutch trailer manufacturer Broshuis for the construction of seven-axle, 65-ton capacity tank transporter trailers, and four-axle, 40-ton capacity heavy equipment trailers. All of the tractor units incorporated 6x6 drive. The 480bhp YTZ95.480s were built to haul the 40-ton trailers, and the 530bhp YTZ95.530s were specified to couple with the 65-ton capacity tank transporter trailers.

All of the tractors were fitted with add-on ballistic kits, specially designed by the Israeli company Plasan Sasa. The first prototypes were ready for testing by mid-2003, and, as a result of extensive field testing, series production commenced on 1st January 2005, with all deliveries completed by the end of the year.

85

In 2002 the Royal Netherlands army placed an order with DAF for 39 6x6 tank transporters with a payload capacity of 65 tons. An additional 63 6x6 heavy transporters with a 40-ton payload capacity, plus ten spare tractors completed the order for what was to become known as the TROPCO system. (Courtesy DAF Trucks NV)

In 2007 Canadian forces deployed German-built Leopard C2 tanks in Kandahar and awaited the arrival of new Leopard 2A6Ms, but neither tank could be moved with existing Canadian 'low boy' trailers. Fortunately, the Dutch army in neighbouring Uruzgan had TROPCOs, which had been specifically designed to transport the 65-ton Leopard 2, and it was able to lease the vehicles to the Canadians for a short time.

Whilst the TROPCO DAFs were the last dedicated military vehicles built at Eindhoven, DAF still considers itself to be in the market for military vehicles, and officially it is still interested in all future military projects.

# DAF goes racing

Like most automotive companies, DAF is no stranger to motor sport. However, whilst a number of its cars were raced and rallied successfully during the 1960s and 70s, its aspirations went upscale in 1982 following the activities of an FAV 1800 DH truck known as the Mighty Mac, which took part in the 1981 Paris-Dakar rally.

In 1982, DAF launched a new bonneted truck, dubbed the N2800, to replace the ill-fated DAF-engined International Paystar 6x4. The new model had been designed from the outset as an on/off-road tipper chassis intended primarily for export markets, such as Africa and the Middle East.

However, while the N-series achieved only limited success in these markets, due to its heavy unladen weight, it did achieve notoriety by being used as a race and support vehicle for the gruelling 1982 Paris-Dakar rally. With veteran car racer and truck operator Jan de Rooy at the wheel, the big DAF actually won first place for vehicles over 10 tons GVW.

Flushed with success, de Rooy and the Dutch DAF dealer team went back for the 1983 event, this time with a purpose-built 320bhp DAF 3300 4x4 truck. Success, however, eluded them; a broken front axle dropped them out of contention, but they were back again the following year with perhaps the most bizarre of all the official DAF Paris-Dakar trucks.

The 1984 DAF 3300 4x4 could almost be accused of not knowing whether it was coming or going. Unofficially dubbed the 'Twin Cabbed Monster' this most bizarre truck had two 400bhp engines, with the front engine driving the rear wheels and the rear engine driving the front wheels. These were mounted in two separate chassis placed one on top of each other. The basic philosophy was that if one engine developed problems the truck could still be driven competitively with the remaining engine.

The twin-engine setup proved tremendously powerful, and so reliable that by the halfway stage not only was the Twin Cab already leading the class for trucks over 10 tons, but it was also running in 32nd place overall in a field of specialist cars and bikes. However, disaster struck, and despite carrying tons of spares the Twin Cab was out of action due to problems with wheel bearings, for which no spares were carried.

In 1985, things eventually came together for Jan de Rooy and DAF Trucks with the construction of another 760bhp, twin-engined 3300 4x4; however, this truck had just one cab. It was dubbed 'the Bull,' and its front-mounted 420bhp DKX engine drove the rear wheels, whilst the rear-mounted 340bhp DKX drove the front wheels.

The Bull achieved first place in the over 10 tons GVW category. Curiously, it could even have been placed in a record-breaking first place overall if it wasn't for penalty points awarded for repairs to panels that had sustained damage in an area where it was too narrow for the safe passage of the truck.

Whilst de Rooy was back again in 1986 with the 1000bhp, purpose-built 3600 Turbo Twin, featuring two centrally mounted twin-turbocharged engines in a steel space frame chassis, tyre problems and a broken hand meant that he did not finish the course. However, not to be outdone, de Rooy was back in 1987 with Turbo Twin II – a truck that was an amazing 1150kg lighter than the previous truck due to its aluminium chassis and components.

Jan de Rooy poses proudly with the 1000bhp Turbo Twin II in which he finished first in the 1987 Paris-Dakar in the category for trucks over 10 tons, coming 11th overall. (Niels Jansen collection)

Luck was with him this time, and he finished first in the category for trucks over 10 tons (some 14.5 hours ahead of the second placed Tatra) and 11th overall. Sadly, the DAF team's luck ran out the following year – a year that initially offered so much promise. For 1988, not one, but two space frame DAF 95s were entered for the Paris-Dakar, numbered X1 and X2.

The X1 could accelerate from 0-100kph in 8.5 seconds and reach a top speed of 180kph. However, on the seventh stage of the event a major accident occurred involving X2, at close to maximum speed. The truck rolled six times, resulting in the death of the 32 year-old navigator, DAF engineer Kees van Loevezijn. DAF immediately pulled out of the event in respect. It never returned to the Paris-Dakar, and the surviving X1 is now displayed at the DAF museum in Eindhoven.

## Circuit racing, too ...

During the 1980s DAF was also involved in the emerging sport of truck racing, although unlike the Paris-Dakar event there were no official factory teams. One of the first truck races in the UK was held in 1984 at Donnington Park race circuit in Derbyshire, and so the nearest DAF dealer – which happened to be Sherwood DAF at Blackwell – was nominated to run a 'dealer team.' However, not only was an ex-demonstrator FT3300 provided to Sherwood, but also the DAF-sponsored Suzuki GP motorcycle world champion Barry Sheene, who embarked on a three-year truck racing stint with the embryonic team.

Peter Bostock, who not only managed the re-engineering of the truck for Sherwood, but often raced the truck as well, recalls that not only did the sport have few rules at the time, but the concept of adapting and tuning a truck for circuit racing was in its infancy. "In our first year we extracted something approaching 400bhp out of the 11.6-litre engine and thought we were doing well," he comments. "However, in 1985 we received a new FT3600, and the first thing we did was to remove the 3600 badge from the front so that we could continue to compete in the up to 350bhp class.

"We'd made a lot of friends in the sport during our

When Sherwood DAF was asked to manage DAF's unofficial participation in European truck racing, it also received GP motorcycle world champion Barry Sheene as driver. (Courtesy Peter Bostock)

When Sherwood received a new FT3600 in 1985 it removed the numerical badges so that it could still compete in the up to 360bhp category. (Courtesy Peter Bostock)

In its third and final truck racing season, Sherwood DAF managed to extract an impressive 630bhp from the 11.6-litre turbo diesel. When the truck was retired from racing at the end of the season, it was returned to factory specification and sold to a local operator. (Courtesy Peter Bostock)

first season of racing and were owed a few favours, so we called one of them in. This allowed us to take the engine, in which we'd changed the pistons and camshaft, to West Coast Diesels – the local agent for Detroit Diesel – and run it on their dynamometer. As a result, we were able to coax some 470bhp out of it, which allowed Barry to race near the front of the pack.

"By 1987 we'd become more experienced with driveline and handling modifications and had tweaked the 11.6-litre engine in another new FT3600 to crank out an impressive 630bhp. Unfortunately, Barry Sheene quit the truck racing scene that year, and after competing in the truck for the balance of the season myself, we took the race truck into the workshop and rebuilt it back to standard road specification. It was acquired the following year by a local operator who

loved to boast that he drove Barry Sheene's old race truck. Which of course he did!"

In the absence of a DAF team, the sport of truck racing grew in stature across Europe, but many were surprised to see DAF return to the sport once again in 1996, competing in the official European Truck Race series. At first the team was not very successful, but in 1997 DAF concluded a deal with Bickel Tuning from Rhinau in Germany for the development and production of DAF race trucks.

With main sponsors Fina Petroleum and Gummi Mayer, the German tyre retreading specialist, on board, Bickel's owner Gerd Körber became both development driver and race truck driver. Using a 12.6-litre sourced from the 95XF and fitted with two Garret turbos, Bickel managed to extract 1250bhp from the DAF diesel at 2600rpm.

Gerd Körber and Alain Ferté campaigned the official DAF Super Racing Trucks team in the late 1990s, racing purpose-built 1250bhp CF race trucks. (Courtesy DAF Trucks Ltd)

French racing legend Alain Ferté later joined DAF's team, and managed to come second in the European Super Truck Racing 1999 season, finishing just 50 points ahead of Gerd Körber. However, with costs mounting and the new DAF management team concentrating on its core business, DAF once more pulled out of truck racing, but then surprised everybody in 2002 by supporting Jan de Rooy's (JDR) refreshed team entry in the Paris-Dakar event.

Gone was the second engine, and the extra turbo had been outlawed under new entry rules. In their place was a single 650bhp turbo engine in a brand new CF85 FAV 4x4 chassis, complete with SISU axles and a Steyr transfer case. The new DAF finished in third place in the 4x4 truck class.

The following year, the JDR team entered two trucks – one driven by Jan, and the other by his son Gerard. Power was increased to 750bhp, which helped Gerard take an early lead in the truck class, but he crashed going over a sand dune. Jan stopped to help his son repair the truck, but such was the performance of the DAF that Jan was still able to finish in 5th place in class.

Gerard's old truck was not raced again, but did appear in the event in 2004 as a back-up truck. Gerard built a brand new race truck with active support from DAF on suspension development, and achieved an overall third place classification.

# The really big stuff – heavy haulage

In the 1950s and 1960s the transport of extra heavy or abnormal-sized loads was the bastion of very specialised operators. Whilst loads had grown in weight and size, the equipment to transport them had not really kept pace. Most haulage companies used a mixture of ex-US army stalwarts from WWII, such as the ubiquitous Diamond T 980/981 series 6x4 tank-transporter tractor, or new specialist trucks from the likes of Scammell, Faun and Willeme. Some hauliers even operated vehicles that had been constructed in the haulier's own workshop, often combining old

A 1984 FT3300 6x4 operated by Chris Bennett Transport of Wilmslow. (Courtesy Bill Clowes)

Super heavyweight 3600 8x4 with Van Seumeren in Holland. (Courtesy Niels Jansen)

military running gear with modern cabs and more powerful diesels.

Whilst many of these specialised transporters often had little more than 200bhp, it was power, or the lack of it, that was a fundamental barrier to progress. In addition, few truckmakers outside of the specialist manufacturers offered 6x4 tractor configurations coupled with high power diesels.

However, all that changed for DAF with the introduction of the F2800 in 1974. With 320bhp SAE available, the big DAF was ideally suited to heavy hauling duties, and was easily capable of hauling gross train weights of 120 tons or more, under abnormal load permits. As the model

progressed through F3300 and F3600 incarnations it proved increasingly popular with heavy haulage operators around the world, who appreciated that it was powerful, rugged and immensely reliable in operation.

Another factor that had an important bearing on the popularity of the big DAF tractor during the late 1970s and throughout the 1980s was the development of the modular multi-axle semi-trailer for abnormal loads. Previously, the design of semi-trailers meant they could rarely carry more than 40 tons, with loads above this weight having to be transported on specially-constructed girder frame trailers pulled by purpose-built ballasted drawbar tractors.

However, as trailer manufacturers applied increasing

This former LC Lewis 95.400 8x4 is moving an historic, 85-ton steam locomotive from Carnforth to Immingham in the livery of Curtis Heavy Haulage. It is seen here with a GTW of 140 tons heading up Clifton Hill in Conisborough.

This unusual, low-cab-forward 95-380 6x2 tractor was specially modified by GINAF to meet Dutch traffic regulations, which require crane booms and jibs to be loaded over the front of the truck. Even the cab roof has been lowered! (Courtesy Harm Adams)

A seriously heavyweight 95XF 530bhp 8x4 operated in Holland. (Courtesy Harm Adams)

levels of technology and innovation to multi-axle modular semi-trailer design, so the motive power requirements shifted in favour of readily-available, high-power, fifth-wheel type semi-tractors, such as the big DAFs.

Whilst the popularity of DAF is constantly increasing among heavy haulage operators across Europe, perhaps one of the most interesting fleets is that operated by Amsterdam-based Koninklijke Saan. This is the largest industrial removal company in the Netherlands, operating a fleet of 80 cranes as well as more than 65 DAF trucks.

Managing director Joop Saan comments: "You can only be in existence for 110 years if you have a good relationship with many loyal customers. In turn, you have to be a loyal customer too. DAF has always been able to meet our needs, and our special transport department has many highly-specialised vehicles, such as a 90-ton 6x4 ballast tractor for a mobile crane and a number of 8x2 trucks with three steering axles."

Operators right across Europe enjoy DAF's combination of high-torque PACCAR diesels and its ability to engineer chassis and axle configurations to meet almost any operational requirement. Here's a selection of images of weird and wonderful DAF heavy haulers doing what they do best.

Amsterdam-based Koninklijke Saan operates some unusual DAFs for industrial removals. Its 8x2 CF, with three steering axles, is seen here bringing KLM's restored DC3 airliner down to earth. (Courtesy Koninklijke Saan)

Low-cab 8x4 CF for hauling long steel structures in Holland. Note the rear of the cab roof has been especially lowered to clear front overhangs. (Courtesy Harm Adams)

Abnormal loads come in all sizes and lengths. This Belgian-registered, long wheelbase CF 430 8x2 tractor and extendable trailer is seen here on the streets of Paris, just after delivering an overlength steel structure. The tractor is equipped with a Gormagh telescopic crane, giving it an unladen weight of 29 tons. (Courtesy Harm Adams)

XF 105-510 6x4 operated by A P Hollingsworth. (Courtesy DAF Trucks Ltd)

Curtis Heavy Haulage took delivery of this 150-ton GVW XF105 FTM 8x4 early in 2009.
(Courtesy Imperial Commercials)

The high torque, 12.9-litre PACCAR MX 510bhp diesel is more than adequate for moving 150-ton GTWs. (Courtesy DAF Trucks NV)

# Recovery trucks

Whilst commercial vehicles slowly grew in size, payload and sophistication in postwar Europe, recovery vehicles – or 'wreckers' as they are sometimes known – often lagged behind in terms of engineering complexity. Most recovery trucks were constructed from vehicles that had come to the end of their normal service life and avoided the cutting torch by being fitted with lifting equipment and maybe a winch or two.

During the late 1940s and early 1950s, the availability of large numbers of war surplus heavyweight trucks, such as AEC, Scammell, Diamond T, Federal, Mack, and Ward Le France 6x4 and 6x6 machines, enabled many recovery operators to gain easy access to capable equipment at a reasonable price. However, whilst these machines were certainly an improvement on the previous generation, their capabilities were soon being stretched, even with retrofits of modern engines and lifting equipment.

As gross vehicle weights edged closer to 40 tons

This 1979, DKS-powered F2800 6x4 is rated at 120 tons GTW, and is fitted with a Boniface Mk1 Interstater and a Holmes 750 hydraulic lifter. It was still working hard in 2009. (Courtesy Mike Glendinning)

across Europe in the 1970s, it became increasingly clear to recovery operations that underpowered and obsolete equipment would no longer do the job. Recovering a heavyweight laden truck and providing a suspended tow at highway speeds required specialist equipment; from a DAF perspective, the launch of the DAF F2800 series in 1974 provided the industry with the perfect tool for the job.

This 3300 6x2, with a non-standard looking second axle, is seen here in Lithuania. Note the creative badging; the ATI logo didn't appear until the introduction of the 3600 series. (Courtesy Max Chern)

The FT2800 in both 4x2 and 6x4 form, together with subsequent heavy duty versions (and even the FAD 8x4 rigid chassis) came as standard with 11.6-litre diesels, including the 320bhp DKS turbocharged and intercooled unit, which could easily handle train weights of over 100 tons with the right gearing. As these trucks became increasingly popular across Europe, pre-owned and then later brand-new chassis became the mainstay of recovery fleets across the UK and Europe.

One of the biggest changes in commercial vehicle recovery happened in the 1970s: the introduction of commercial recovery associations. These based themselves loosely on the tried and tested formula set by the increasingly popular private car motoring associations.

At the end of 1972, DAF was the first truck manufacturer to launch an international assistance service that stranded drivers could call for help. This unique emergency aid scheme was branded as the International Truck Service (ITS),

The shape of things to come. This 430bhp, 95XF with purpose-built recovery bodywork is a far cry from the ex-army equipment that was the mainstay of the European recovery industry just a couple of decades earlier. (Courtesy Mark Carnevale)

Aberystwyth-based RecoverMyTruck used its own in-house facilities to build this unique 10x4 CF. (Courtesy Lee Coulson)

Specialist truck builder GINAF is best known for using DAF cabs, engines and axles on its 10x8 dump trucks, so this huge recovery truck with four steering axles is something of a monster. (Courtesy Niels Jansen)

also known as DAF Service Partner in Germany and DAFaid in the UK. The philosophy behind the launch of ITS was simply that as a provider of high-quality transport equipment, DAF should be supporting this with the establishment and maintenance of a high-quality service organisation.

Calls to the ITS central helpline are answered by operators, each of whom speaks at least four languages. Assistance is not limited to the vehicle only; it is also provided for the trailer, the load, and even the driver.

Recovery operators selected to become part of the ITS team make it their task to get stranded DAF trucks back on the road within 24 hours – a goal that was achieved in 90 per cent of cases right from day one.

In the UK, DAFaid uses one central telephone number, manned by experts 24/7. When first launched, the service set a new bench mark in vehicle support by providing not only the expected emergency recovery and repair service, but also information on lorry parks, overnight accommodation, ferry bookings and even the location of the nearest refrigerated warehouse. DAFaid also comprehensively covers every DAF truck being used on British roads and every British DAF truck in operation across Europe.

Historically, many recovery operators constructed their own DAF-based recovery vehicles, often re-using lifting and winching equipment taken from older vehicles in the fleet that have been decommissioned. Some even carried out their own major chassis surgery, including wheelbase

Typical of 21st century recovery trucks, this is an impressive CF85 8x4 with 510bhp and a GTW of some 150 tons. (Courtesy Colin Ryan)

modifications and adding axles to help cope with the increased axle loadings imposed when giving a suspended tow to a 40+ton truck.

Whilst modern highway trucks have to comply with strict regulations in construction, use, and type approval, recovery vehicles are permitted to operate outside of these rules. Therefore, they are allowed to have 'modifications' that would be deemed illegal on highway trucks. However, whilst many of these re-engineered trucks may be visually impressive, DAF also has a long history of being protective of the structural integrity of its trucks and how they are used, thus safeguarding its reputation.

Today, DAF is set up to build over 99 per cent of its trucks to a standardised type approval format, that complies with 48 different European directives and regulations concerning specification and vehicle types. Tony Pain, marketing director of DAF in the UK, comments, "We actually build over 23 million different variants of model specifications 'as standard' and these cover 99 per cent of the truck market, and are, by definition, 'approved variants.'

"However, there are still operators that require something special, and we do indeed build special trucks on a 'bespoke basis' – for instance with a unique wheelbase, as we like to build the truck 'right first time' where possible. So, whilst we are not in a position to formally approve conversions which take place after the chassis is built, we do work with numerous specialist bodybuilders to try and ensure that any appropriate retro-conversion is legal, reliable and durable."

The installation of additional axles, especially where it involves changes to the braking system, are almost non-existent these days because of type approval regulations. Indeed, it tends to be only those who operate outside of normal regulations who still do conversions – none of which can be 'factory approved' because DAF has not actually tested them.

Tony Pain concludes, "We try to build enough model variants in order to reduce the number of conversions that are done these days, and we certainly do not promote the concept of conversions, whether to chassis, engine or axles."

XF105 6x2 with 510bhp. (Courtesy DAF Trucks Ltd)

CF85 6x2 with pusher axle. (Courtesy Niels Jansen)

# Overseas round-up

Today, DAF products are sold and serviced by a network of more than 1000 independent dealer locations throughout Europe, the Middle East, Africa, Australia, New Zealand and Taiwan. Global sales exceeded 60,000 units in 2007 and the company is continuing to expand in Central and Eastern Europe.

However, its increasing global presence has been conducted in a carefully orchestrated expansion plan following sales successes in the Benelux and the UK. For instance, 1994 was a good year for the 85 series, being voted UK Fleet Truck of the Year, and towards the end of the year a factory for the assembly of the series was set up in Casablanca, Morocco.

These trucks were destined for export throughout North Africa and the Middle East, including Iraq. A year after the opening of the Moroccan plant, it was announced that the 85 series would

One of the first DAF 3600s sold in Australia went to Andrews Transport, where it clocked up more than 3.2 million kilometres before being sold out of service. Apparently it's still working as a dump truck! (Courtesy Richard Mohr)

be assembled in China by the Chanfeng Auto Corporation, and the year after that saw the official opening of the DAF subsidiary in Warsaw, Poland.

Although small numbers of DAFs had made their way to Australia in the late 1980s and early 1990s, things were put on a firmer footing in 1998 with the formation of DAF Trucks Australia as a division of PACCAR Australia Pty Ltd.

The Australian heavy truck industry is a well established user of large American-based trucks, such as the PACCAR-built Kenworth. However, many operators had bad experiences of European truckmakers selling trucks in Australia; some offered poor service support, and then pulled out when things got tough, often leaving the operators with virtually worthless vehicles.

The very first 3600 space cab in Australia was this truck operated by Allan Copini, who specialised in hauling refrigerated goods between Adelaide, Melbourne and Sydney. Of Dutch descent, Allan visited the Eindhoven factory on a visit to the homeland in 1987, and was in awe of the new space cab. He made such an impression on factory employees that, when the first space cab arrived in Australia, they called him. Allan didn't hesitate and purchased it there and then, and it was presented to him at the Sydney Truck Show in 1987. (Courtesy Allan Copini)

So, DAF's early years in Australia were mostly spent researching market trends and developing vehicle specifications that met Australia's demanding conditions, as well as training and appointing sales and after-sales support staff.

Following the introduction of the LF and the new CF at the beginning of the millennium, both models were selected for assembly in Australia. Whilst initial sales were slow, DAF Trucks Australia reached an important milestone in 2005 with the delivery of its one thousandth truck to an operator in Queensland. By the end of 2008 sales had exceeded 2000 vehicles, and a network of 32 dealers had been put in place to support the future growth of DAF 'Down Under'.

DAF has also been active in Taiwan since 2006 and has steadily built a reputation based on reliability and low operating costs. With a fleet of more than 135 DAF trucks, Formosa Plastics Transport Corporation (FPTC) is the single largest customer of DAF in Taiwan, and not without reason. The company is part of Formosa Plastics Group (FPG), which is one of the largest petrochem companies in the world, and the world's largest producer of PVC.

This 8x4 CF tractor in Australia demonstrates the DAF's dual ability as a crane truck and load carrier. (Courtesy DAF Trucks Australia)

DAF is steadily making inroads into the construction industry in Australia, and this 10x4 CF is typical of the trucks spearheading the campaign.
(Courtesy DAF Trucks Australia)

Seiko Chen, executive director of FPTC, took the decision to standardise his fleet of approximately 600 trucks, of various makes, on DAF. Mr Chen also has a senior role with FPG, where he is responsible for the import, assembly and sales of DAF trucks throughout the region. So, what better advertisement for the product than to introduce it into one of the largest trucking fleets in Taiwan?

Currently, up to ten CFs are built up from CKD kits each week in FPG's modern assembly facility. Workers have all been trained by DAF to ensure the quality of the finished product is equal to that coming out of the plants in Eindhoven and Leyland. As a result of FPG's pioneering venture, DAF is slowly gaining an enviable reputation amongst Taiwanese operators, and by the end of 2008 almost 450 DAFs were trucking around the island. "Japanese brands currently have the majority of the market here, mainly due to their low initial purchase price," says Mr Chen. "However, a low operating cost per kilometre is becoming an increasingly important factor and nobody scores better than DAF in that respect."

After earning the International Truck of the Year 2007 accolade, DAF's top-of-the-range XF105 garnered the Truck of the Year distinction in Poland for the second consecutive year. In Ireland, the XF105 was honoured by *Fleet Transport* magazine as Irish Tractor of the Year, as well as Irish Truck of the Year 2007.

With the assistance of PACCAR, DAF has become the leading truck manufacturer in Europe today, and is steadily making inroads into a large number of overseas markets. European Union truck registration figures for 2007 reveal that in the 6 to 15-ton sector DAF's share was 8.3 per cent, mainly as a result of the decline of the UK market, where DAF is market leader. In the over 15-ton sector, 2007 market demand actually exceeded production capacity, despite increased production and record deliveries of almost 50,000 heavy trucks (11 per cent more than in 2006). This resulted in an overall market share of 13.9 per cent across Western Europe.

In the Netherlands, one out of every three heavyweight trucks sold in 2007 was a DAF, whereas in the UK one out

This battered 380bhp CF A-train double trailer outfit is seen here in Russia operating a regular service to Finland. (Courtesy Max Chern)

of every four trucks sold was a DAF. Around this time, DAF was further enhancing its presence in Germany – the largest truck market in Europe – where its share of the over 15-ton market increased to 9.7 per cent. In France, DAF achieved a market share of 12.8 per cent; in Italy 9.7 per cent; in Spain 11.2 per cent, and in Belgium 18.6 per cent.

By 2008, DAF further strengthened its position in Western Europe from 13.7 to 14.0 per cent overall, with sizeable gains in its major markets of France, Belgium and Luxemburg, Germany, and the Netherlands. Market share in the UK dropped from 26.3 per cent to 25.1 per cent with further reductions in Italy and Spain. However, growth in sales in the Central European market saw DAF's stake rise to 14.6 per cent overall during 2008, with significant slices of the Polish (19.4 per cent) and Slovakian (15 per cent) truck markets.

Heavy haul and extra long-haul! This 95XF is seen here after hauling a Grove RT890E crane from Mombasa to Kampala, Uganda – a journey that took the best part of three weeks to complete. It's coupled to a 100-ton Nicolas modular trailer. (Courtesy Jerry Burley)

The strong position of DAF in the major markets of Germany, France, Spain and Italy is important for DAF's geographical diversity of sales. Ten years ago, DAF's traditional markets – the UK and the Benelux – accounted for some three quarters of total sales, with the balance going to Germany and Southern Europe.

In recent years, DAF has strengthened its position in both Central and Eastern Europe, as well as international markets such as Australia, Taiwan, New Zealand, South Africa and the Middle East, and with the assistance of parent company PACCAR it is continually exploring new markets and opportunities.

DAF is proving increasingly popular in New Zealand, where 44-ton GVW outfits require eight axles.
(Courtesy Southpac Trucks)

95 and 85 series eight-axle livestock haulers in New Zealand. (Courtesy Rod Simmons)

XF95-530 eight-axle B-train outfit in New Zealand. (Courtesy Rod Simmons)

XF105-510 44-ton eight-axle drawbar outfit in New Zealand. (Courtesy Rod Simmons)

85CF 8x4 concrete mixer in Israel. (Courtesy David T Sodikoff)

# Supply of components

Although DAF may not be regarded as a mainstream supplier of components to other manufacturers, such as those in the construction, marine, or even automotive industries, the Eindhoven operation does, in fact, have a rich history of supplying such things, and it's a tradition that's still carrying on today.

One company that has been using DAF components for many years is the Dutch specialist vehicle builder GINAF, which started installing DAF diesels into refurbished ex-US army REO 6x6s in the 1960s, then converting them into dump trucks. As sales increased, GINAF became a certified truck builder in its own right and began using DAF axles and cabs. It even took to converting and modifying standard DAF trucks to meet specific customer requirements.

Today, GINAF builds a wide range of trucks using its own chassis, hydraulic suspension and steering axles, but it has a strong focus on on/off-highway trucks, which can operate up to 50 tons GVW in Holland. This is a both a specialised and niche market that requires production of just 150-200 trucks a year when the economy is strong. So, it is not a market that would be viable for DAF to enter itself.

In Holland, many DAF dealers also sell GINAF products alongside those from Eindhoven. Additionally, DAF also supplied engines to specialist Belgian off-road truck builder MOL.

Whilst the partial marriage to International Harvester in 1973 witnessed the birth of a number of hybrid trucks, comprising both DAF and IH components, it was perhaps the sale of the range-topping F241 cab – from the F2800 series – to the Hungarian manufacturer RABA that really established DAF as an international component supplier. The cabs were supplied by DAF in a fully-assembled condition, and were installed on 4x2 and 6x2 tractors and a variety of rigid trucks, many of which were used by the state-owned Hungarocamion trucking organisation to transport freight across Europe.

Another area where DAF quietly excelled was in the supply of diesel engines. DAF had formed a relationship with Leyland back in the 1950s for the supply of British-built diesels, which were later re-designed and built in Eindhoven. Early in 1986, DAF started an intensive co-operation programme with British Leyland that resulted in the supply of DAF-built 8.25-litre engines for Leyland to install in the Leyland Constructor.

DAF trucks and their component parts have been converted into some amazing machinery in recent years. An obscure French company using the brand TITAN (not to be confused with the Germany company of the same name, which builds heavy haulage machinery) constructed a most unusual machinery carrier for Bonal & Fils in Paris. This highly odd machine uses a DAF CF 85 cab and a 430bhp DAF diesel to power the front steering axle, as the rest of the truck can be hydraulically lowered to the ground.

Another strange group of DAF-based trucks were built by the Dutch company Van der Kooij in Rotterdam in the late 1980s and early 1990s, under the brand KAF, which stood for Kooij Automobiel Fabriek. All were five-axle rigids rated at 46 tons GVW, and it is believed that two were assembled using 3300/3600 components, whilst three more were based on the DAF CF85.

This filthy but hard-working 10x6 GINAF dump truck is the company's top-of-the-range X 5376 T model.

Hungarian truck maker RABA used DAF F241 cabs on a wide range of tractor units and trucks during the late 1970s

GINAF is not the only Dutch truck manufacture to have used DAF components. Schiedam-based Kooij Automobiel Fabriek built a handful of 3600- and CF85-based KAF 10x6 tankers during the late 1980s and early 1990s. (Courtesy Niels Jansen)

This bizarre 8x2 truck uses a DAF cab and 430bhp diesel to power the front steering axle. Manufactured in France by the little-known Titan outfit, the bed of the truck can be hydraulically lowered to the ground for loading heavy machinery items. (Courtesy Harm Adams)

The C500 is classified as the serious workhorse of the Kenworth line-up, with GTWs of up to 200 tons and diesels up to 600bhp. This unusual hybrid sports a DAF XF 105 cab, and maybe points the way for future component sharing between DAF and fellow PACCAR stablemates. (Courtesy Niels Jansen collection)

# Restoring for the future

DAF is unusual amongst truck manufacturers in that not only does it have numerous clubs around the world, dedicated to the preservation and restoration of its cars and trucks, but it also has its own purpose-built museum.

Opened in 1990, at Tongelresestraat 27 in Eindhoven on the site of the original DAF workshops, the museum houses the most comprehensive and historically-important collection of DAF products to be found anywhere in the world. Staffed by volunteers made up mostly of ex-DAF employees, the museum has its own restoration workshop where suitable vehicles are dismantled and restored to show quality. A visit to the museum is surely a must for anybody with even a remote interest in DAF trucks.

In 1951 DAF introduced a pickup truck: the A107 and the A117 with a longer wheelbase. Powered by a 91bhp Hercules JXE-3 petrol engine, it was sold as a chassis/cowl with a steel cab an optional extra. The little DAF trucks were mainly used by overseas oil companies, with many operated by the Dutch authorities in Western New Guinea. Recently, the remains of two trucks were repatriated from Curacao and rebuilt into one new truck in the DAF Museum. Sadly, the little DAF cannot be used on public roads, as the original pickup never received Dutch type approval, and consequently cannot be registered.

The DAF museum in Eindhoven operates a fully functional restoration shop where trucks like this 1962 T1300 are rebuilt to as-new condition.

# Also from Veloce –

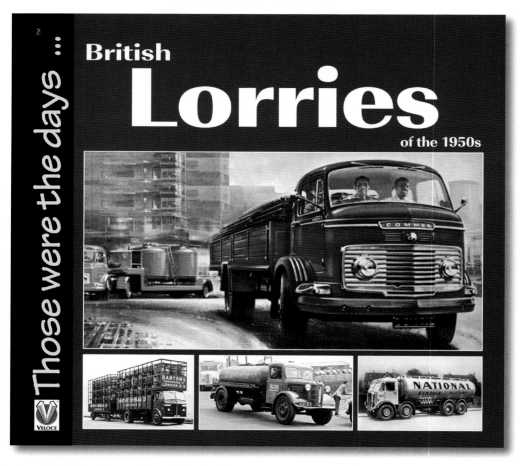

A highly visual look at British lorries produced during the austere 1950s. Familiar and less familiar names connected with the road haulage industry are covered, with comprehensive text revealing much about these productive and essential vehicles.

**£14.99**
**ISBN: 978-1-84584-209-3**

For more info on Veloce titles, visit our website at www.veloce.co.uk
email info@veloce.co.uk • tel: +44 (0)1305 260068 • prices subject to change • p+p extra

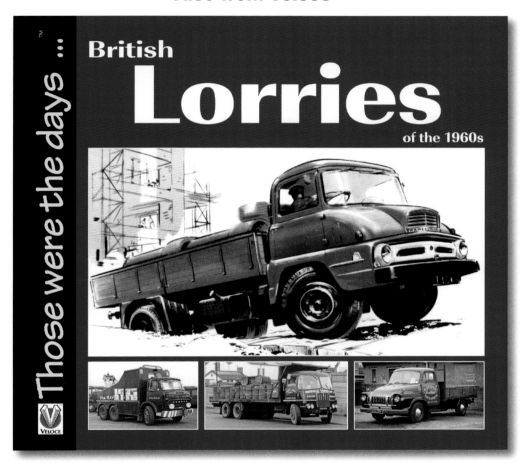

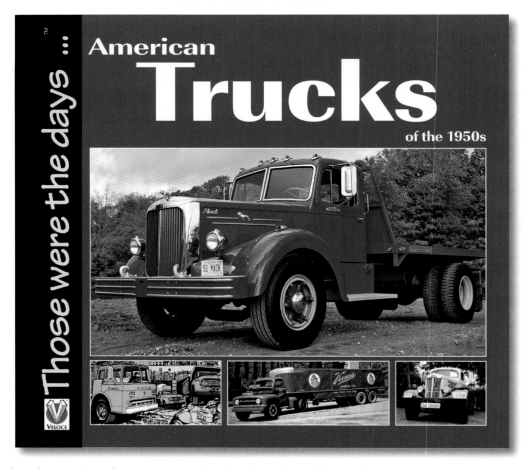

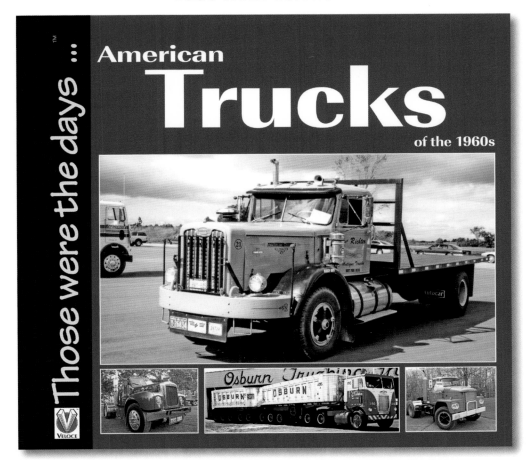

# Index